MW01452620

Thinking Ahead
Toward the Next Generation of Judaism

Oskar Brecher

Thinking Ahead
Toward the Next Generation of Judaism

A Collection of Essays
By
Contemporary Reform Rabbis and Scholars
In honor of Oskar Brecher
President of Temple Israel of the City of New York
1995 – 2000

Rabbi Judith S. Lewis
Editor

Keshet Press
Binghamton, New York
2001

Copyright © 2001 by Rabbi Judith S. Lewis

All rights reserved. No portion of this publication may be duplicated in any way without the expressed written consent of the publisher, except in the form of brief excerpts or quotations for the purpose of review.

Printed in the United States of America.

Keshet Press
9 Riverside Drive
Binghamton, New York 13905
Phone: (607) 723-7355
Fax: (607) 723-0785
E-mail: KeshetBks@aol.com
Web: http://www.tier.net/keshetpress

Distributed by Global Publications
LNG 99, Binghamton University
State University of New York
Binghamton, New York 13902-6000
Phone: (607) 777-4495 or 6104; Fax: (607) 777-6132
E-mail: pmorewed@binghamton.edu
http://ssips.binghamton.edu

ISBN 1-892006-07-3

Preface

Oskar Brecher became president of Temple Israel of the City of New York because of his Herculean efforts in restoring the external physical integrity of our building, as chairman of the House Committee. He claimed, when he agreed to accept the presidency, that his interest in the "religious" side of Judaism was limited, but that he would help the congregation in any way he could, out of a sense of obligation to the community. Despite his protestations, Oskar Brecher quickly became a leading advocate for restoring the intellectual and spiritual integrity of Reform Judaism. His knowledge of Jewish texts and history gives him a level of credibility unusual among the lay leadership of our movement. He has pushed us to probe beyond the surface of popular Jewish trends, to articulate a coherent philosophical approach for modern Jews.

Each of the authors in this volume has emerged as an important partner of Temple Israel in this quest for a viable modern Judaism. I extend my deepest gratitude to each of them for participating in this publication, and for sharing our journey.

Oskar Brecher has observed that the work of a Temple president is ephemeral and leaves behind no lasting mark as the institution continues to move forward. I do not usually disagree with him – and certainly not publicly – but in this case I know that he is wrong. Not only will he have permanently transformed the physical appearance and effectiveness of our building, but he has also permanently transformed how we think about our lives as members of the Jewish community. This volume is the proof – and we offer it to him in gratitude for his

THINKING AHEAD

constant support and encouragement. We hope that it will provide food for serious thought and discussion among its readers, and motivate others to join us in this quest for a meaningful, living Judaism for our children and our children's children.

Judith S. Lewis
Senior Rabbi

Tribute

During the tenure of Oskar Brecher as President of Temple Israel, every aspect of our educational program was "reformed." One of his first efforts was to add another rabbi to our staff, to increase our ability to serve the families of our congregation. In the succeeding year, we retained new directors for our Nursery School and Religious School as well. In a very short time, these dedicated individuals have revitalized the quality of education provided to the children and adults of our congregation. Their work is the practical application of many of the ideas presented in this volume, and while their primary tribute to Oskar Brecher takes place every day in our classrooms, we wanted to preserve a record of their participation in our efforts by including these dedications:

A Man of Intellect

When I was a soon-to-be-ordained student preparing to interview for the position of Assistant Rabbi at Temple Israel, I read a brief description of the temple that the search committee had written. To the amazement of every student rabbi who was reading job descriptions, Temple Israel was the only congregation to use the German phrase *Wissenschaft des Judentums*. "The Scientific Study of the Jewish religion" was the intellectual foundation of Reform Judaism in its earliest days in Germany. And here I was about to sit before our Temple's president and it's Senior Rabbi trying to persuade them to hire me.

THINKING AHEAD

More intimidating even than Temple Israel's commitment to the highest standard of Reform Judaism's intellectual foundation and its rich heritage as a Classical Reform Congregation of German Jews, was Oskar Brecher sitting across from me. Not being able to decipher his accent or country of origin from our conversation, I imagined that Temple Israel was so well grounded in its classical German roots that their President was yet another example of their commitment to Wissenschaft.

My experience at Temple Israel may not serve me well if I go from here to lead a congregation of my own. This is a very special place, and I am fearful that there is not another congregation like it. What will happen when I go from here and find that not every temple board functions as smoothly as ours? In my three years here I cannot recall a single instance when our president's gavel was needed. Oskar Brecher has led this congregation with dignity and integrity.

Temple Israel has grown both physically and programmatically under Oskar's stewardship. Every floor of our building reflects a physical improvement that Oskar has made possible. Moreover, the building that is beginning to take a new shape around us is overflowing with programming activity.

In the Talmud we are asked the rhetorical question of whether it is possible to build a house between heaven and earth. The Talmud answers that only God can accomplish such a task. Anyone who has worked with Oskar Brecher, however, knows that an answer like that will only incite him to prove it wrong. Those of us who have watched the evolution of Temple Israel under his presidency realize that the word "impossible" is not in Oskar Brecher's vocabulary.

Howard I. Needleman
Associate Rabbi

TRIBUTES

A Man of Action

I first met Oskar Brecher after my final meeting with the Nursery School Search Committee. He was in Rabbi Lewis' office, a thick file folder in front of him. As we talked, he signed letter after letter. I was impressed with his powers of concentration, never missing a beat in the conversation, never pausing in his letter signing. He was extremely focused – extremely sure of himself, yet genuinely interested in our meeting. It was immediately apparent that the health and well being of the Nursery School were of primary concern to him. He was fully aware of the needed administrative and programming changes. I was not only excited by the challenges my new position here presented but was delighted to realize that changes would have the full support of the Temple Board. Oskar Brecher clearly had a vision for the school, fully realizing how the improvement of the school would affect the life of the temple.

When parents comment on the revisions and transformation of the school, they should realize that none could have taken place without the full support of Oskar Brecher and the Board of Trustees.

Nancy-Ellen Micco, Director
Early Childhood Learning Center

A Man of Vision

I first met Oskar Brecher during my interview for the position of Religious School Director. He spoke of the goals and vision he had for the Religious School, letting me know the school was a priority. He has been supportive, interested in the progress of the school, and helpful in implementing changes. He understands the importance of Jewish education and its impact upon the future of the Jewish community. Oskar Brecher connects the success of Jewish learning with the environment in which it is taking place. He has been instrumental in ensuring sufficient resources for us, and has had ongoing personal involvement with the school, helping to create an environment that is bright, energized and makes children feel warm and welcome. Any individual entering our space will now know that serious, fun Jewish learning is taking place here.

There is a teaching in Pirke Avot – The Ethics of Our Fathers that currently hangs on our Religious School wall under the "Thought for the Month" sign. It says:

> "It is not your job to finish the work, but you are not free to walk away from it."

Oskar Brecher has certainly taken this teaching seriously. He has given himself to Temple Israel for five years, and has made this place a part of "his job." He has created a vision for what Temple Israel should be now and in the future, even at a time when he will no longer be its president. He is not responsible to "finish the work," but he has done more than his share to begin it. Oskar Brecher has demonstrated an exemplary model of leadership and hard work for the rest of us to learn from and emulate in the future.

Jennifer Katz, Director
Religious School

The work of a Temple President is never finished, but the quality of one's successor is an important indication of how much has been accomplished. We are proud and delighted to be able to include these words of tribute from the person who will now take on the mantle of leadership of Temple Israel of the City of New York.

TRIBUTES

Tribute to Oskar Brecher

Oskar Brecher is a hard act to follow! His leadership, hard work and dedication to Temple Israel will have a profoundly positive effect on all of us for many years to come. What a fine foundation he has put in place: he leaves the presidency with every aspect of our beloved temple in the best condition it could be, and with great a feeling of optimism on the part of the entire congregation. And, he has accomplished all of this with a positive attitude, a great sense of purpose and an even greater sense of humor. He has set a standard that I can only hope to approach in my tenure.

In addition, I would like to express my heartfelt gratitude to his wife, Adrienne, whose patience and understanding allowed him to give so much of himself to us. It is truly an honor to have come to know them both as cherished friends.

Martin Cohen, President-Elect
December 11, 2000

CONTENTS

MY JOURNEY IN JUDAISM
    Oskar Brecher   1

WHAT ARE THE BASIC PRINCIPLES OF REFORM JUDAISM?
    Robert M. Seltzer and Lance J. Sussman   7

THE SQUARE ROOT OF 10,000 Or When is 100 not 100?
    Leonard Kravitz   17

INTERPRETING THE AKEDAH YEAR BY YEAR
    Robert M. Seltzer   39

ABRAHAM AND THE IDOLS
    Robert B. Barr   69

COMING HOME TO GLOBAL JUDAISM
    Lance J. Sussman   73

A NEW JEWISH AWAKENING
    Samuel N. Gordon   81

PEACE AND THE RELIGIOUS QUESTION
    Uri Regev   95

CAUSING REASONED REACTIONS
    Judith S. Lewis   103

MY JOURNEY IN JUDAISM

Oskar Brecher

My *bris* in early August of 1945 was widely celebrated according to my father. If legend be true, I was the first male baby born in Szatmar, Transylvania after the war. After the destruction of the one hundred-year-old Jewish community in just three days in May of 1944, unbeknownst to me, I became a symbol. Barely 2000 Jews returned to Szatmar and my birth, I was told, was the first faint hope of rebirth.

The Szatmar of the late 1940's and 1950's was more akin to living in the 19th Century. Instead of nursery school, I went to *cheder* and I continued after elementary school every day. On Wednesdays I often accompanied my mother to the market for a goose and then on to the ritual slaughterhouse. The *shochet* would come to the window of his booth, examine the bird and dispatch it with a deft stroke of the blade. Thursday mornings we would take the braided dough to a local bakery to bake the *challah*. On Friday, I would bicycle over with the *tcholent*. Friday, early afternoon, it was off to the *mikvah* the size of a major swimming pool. Steam rooms and massages were also available.

Friday night our world was hermetically sealed. Off to *shul* we went, where my father had an *aliyah* every week because he was the only surviving *Cohen*. And if a "big" Rebbe came from Kolozsvár or Bucharest we paid him a visit on Saturday afternoon. It was a warm and comforting existence.

Slowly I become aware of the issues that twisted the fault lines of our small town. I was a good pioneer. I wore my red silk neckerchief daily and cheered the triumphs of communism such as the launching of the Sputnik. All the while I tried to reconcile the promise of the inevitable utopia with the show trial of all local Jewish managers of a state enterprise, my father among the defendants.

Szatmar was also a civilized little town where each child was expected to study music, drawing and languages. I still remember the arguments about the Second Coming between my father and my French tutor, who happened to be a Catholic priest, with his ingrained, good natured, persistently relentless, anti-Semitism.

In 1958, we made *aliyah* to Israel. It was a country that was still raw and unformed. Barbed wire from the British Mandate days was strung everywhere. There were daily incidents of violence – a shooting into the German donated passenger train between Jerusalem and Tel Aviv with its large windows, not more than ten feet from the Armistice line; another shooting ten feet from the Mandelbaum Gate. And there were triumphs such as Eichman being captured in Argentina and starting his journey to Israel rolled up in a Persian carpet. I heard that bit of news on the radio while on an overnight camping trip on the beaches of Ashkelon. Diesel spewing Egged buses choked the air, straining with crowds of heavily accented Hebrew speaking immigrants. Yet every fifteen minutes there was dead silence on the bus as the Kol Israel news broadcast was absorbed by everyone.

We lived in a concrete block *shikun* with no electricity. I did my homework by kerosene lamp. At home and at school we were close to the earth. We were constantly hauling dirt in rubber baskets, building acres (dunams) of terraces. You could not help but be caught up in the penetrating tidal wave of socialist Zionist sentiment.

The Torah that I studied in Romania in Yiddish translation as a fundamental religious text became utterly transformed.

It turned into poetry whose very sounds properly pronounced had an irresistible cadence. The softly rolled *reish*, the *ayin* from the throat gave me palpable pleasure. With a Talmud tutor, I had a daily dose of *Baba Metziah* or *Baba Kama* – but this time in Hebrew translation. I remember listening raptly to the radio when *Tanach* contests were the equivalent of "Who Wants to be a Millionaire." I became completely immersed in Jewish history, Jewish customs and traditions, Hebrew grammar and Hebrew and Zionist literature. Inevitably, I became well-grounded in Jewish knowledge.

As remarkably internally consistent as my life was in Israel, inconsistencies would simmer to the surface. I listened to the vituperative hatred of anything Israeli by my second cousin Getzel, well trapped in the snares of the *Neturei Carta*. I marveled at the remarkable wealth of those most closely associated with the Vishinitzer Rebbe. One of his followers bid the princely sum of 400 liras (about $10,000 today) for the privilege of reading *Maftir Yonah* on Yom Kippur in the Rebbe's grand synagogue – a service I attended in 1959. Nachum Brecher, a Chasidic first cousin of my father's and *gabbai* of the Rebbe managed to parlay a fish store and a side business in polished diamonds into a very comfortable life.

Most interestingly, in Israel I ceased to be a Jew. I was Jewish all right – but then so was everyone else. While in Romania I was always a Jew, in Israel I was, with the deepest irony, a Romanian. Being Romanian was the lower middle rung of the social totem pole below Hungarians and Poles with the *Yekes* and Anglo Saxons occupying the top perch.

Fast forward to Canada in the 1960's and 1970's. We arrived with 3 Canadian dollars into the waiting arms of my uncle in Montreal. For the first few months we lived a Mordechai Richler life. We shared an apartment with another family on L'Esplanade just a block from Richler's famed St. Urbain Street. The daughter of the family was a receptionist at HIAS (Hebrew

Immigrants Assistance Society) and she was reveling in her newly purchased electric typewriter.

As many immigrants, I saw my arrival in Canada as the opportunity to shed my Old World existence. Even my name had changed from Oscar in Romania, to Yehudah in Israel, to Oskar in Canada as it was retransliterated from the Hebrew אוסקר by the Canadian Embassy.

I attended *shul* as rarely as possible – taking long walks during the reading of the Torah at Kasherer Dayan's *shtibl* where my father went. After my mother died in 1963, I was largely AWOL from Young Israel – our new *shul*.

I spent six years at McGill University in the Architecture program. Under the legendary art and architectural historian and critic P.C. Collins, aesthetic appreciation -- the interactions of humans in spatial volumes -- and the details of manufacturing space became my new paramount interest. There is a story, perhaps apocryphal, that a group of orthodox rabbis was invited to visit an art exhibit. At the conclusion of their tour they were asked how they enjoyed it. They responded that they were extremely impressed by the informative, articulate and authoritative captions. By contrast, I was beginning to see the art.

My secular transformation was completed at Harvard Business School. Here I was taught a different form of art, perhaps even a religion. I had by now traveled through many "isms" to this bastion of Capitalism.

I could have easily persisted in this mode for the rest of my life had I not married and had a son. Suddenly that formative theme of Jewish continuity resurfaced. I could not go back to Orthodox Judaism, nor could secular Zionism be a logical path in America.

I was searching for a way to fulfill an unarticulated obligation that I should raise my son as a Jew. The Nursery School at Temple Israel in Manhattan seemed to fill the bill. It was merely four blocks from our apartment, the closest nursery school. We joined the Temple. The first High Holidays proved to be an exercise in radical culture shock. Here I was, seeking to provide Jewish continuity for my son, and finding instead another totally foreign expression of religious observance.

Over time, however, I began to carve out a space for myself in Reform Judaism, with the encouragement of Rabbi Lewis and the other religious leaders who contributed to this book and share her vision. There is no easy or comfortable path to a modern and meaningful Judaism. It is all too tempting to succumb to a "Judaism Lite," as Robert Seltzer in his now famous sound bite referred to it – a less demanding, ritualistic traditionalism replete with all the trappings of my childhood religious experience. But it is not clear to me that such a superficial solution will provide the kind of continuity I would like to pass on to future generations.

Throughout my five years as President of Temple Israel, I have tried to support efforts to create a progressive Judaism that will appeal both to the intellects and the emotions of our membership. Our community is made up of individuals who would never settle for anything less than the finest in their food, clothing, shelter, or any other material acquisitions. I want to insure that we can offer them the very finest **spiritual** food, clothing, and shelter as well. They should not have to be satisfied with a pale imitation of the traditional Judaism of my youth.

For me, it would be hard to conceive of a Judaism not based on a thorough knowledge of Jewish text, Jewish tradition and Jewish history. Only then can we identify the philosophical underpinnings and ethical values that arise from our tradition. Those values and principles have had a tremendous transformative power on generation after generation. In 2500 years, through radically diverse historical, social, economic, and political challenges, they have not failed to provide a living Judaism for our ancestors.

We have been to the brink many times, as a people, and

each time managed to transform the very hopelessness of our position into the new foundation of our renewal.

    By sheer accident, I have witnessed a large arc of the modern Jewish experience. Without any intentional consciousness, I have absorbed much more of it than I perhaps realized as I was living through it. As I see my name connected to this volume of essays, by individuals who have become friends and colleagues as a result of my involvement in the Reform Movement, I think back to the year of my birth. In 1946 my father, who was an eternal optimist, saw me as a promise to fulfill his hope for Jewish continuity. In an entirely unpredictable way, I have found myself working to realize his dream. I think he would be pleased.

WHAT ARE THE BASIC PRINCIPLES OF REFORM JUDAISM?

Robert M. Seltzer and Lance J. Sussman

Background

The Central Conference of American Rabbis, in May 1999 in Pittsburgh at the climax of its annual convention, adopted a new "Statement of Principles" the fourth of a series of formal declarations that began with the Pittsburgh Platform of 1885. The previous summer, when the first drafts of the new statement were being circulated, I was asked by the editor of Reform Judaism, *the magazine published by the Union of American Hebrew Congregations, to respond to the proposal. My critique was published in the next issue, together with a defense of the proposed official statement by Rabbi Richard Levy, its author.[1] I argued that Rabbi Levy's document failed to convey the distinctive and ongoing mission of the Reform movement, that it placed far too much emphasis on religious ceremony at the expense of ethics, that it exploited venerable Hebrew religious terminology, such as* mitzvah, kedushah, *and* brit, *without trying to indicate what these terms mean to us now, and that it ignored the great strides that Reform Judaism had made over the last two centuries in demonstrating the compatibility of Judaism with modern scientific and historical truth. While the practice of Reform Judaism certainly involved personal and communal rit-*

---

[1] "This is Not the Way," *Reform Judaism* vol. 27, no.. 2 (Winter 1998), 23-26, 80. The title is borrowed from the historic essay by Ahad Ha-Am, the spokesman for Cultural Zionism, against the short-sighted efforts of the Love of Zion movement in Russia in the late 1880s.

ual, prayer, and respect for tradition, and while it was committed to the survival of the Jewish religion and the Jewish people, I insisted that it should not do so at the expense of an outward-looking vision of Judaism's public role in modern society. I warned that "we must guard against turning Reform Judaism into Conservative Judaism Lite" which, as my older daughter noted, was the only sound-bite that had ever popped up in my writing and a phrase that was quoted in the media during the extended debate over the new principles.

On June 14 1999, I was invited by Rabbi Lewis to discuss some of these issues at a meeting of the Board of Temple Israel. I criticized the implication of those defending the new platform that Reform Judaism lacked "authenticity" (a term notoriously difficult to define with precision) and that the answer was "traditionalism" (a concept which is more emotional rather than rational). Instead, I argued, what was needed was a reaffirmation of the role of critical reason in discerning which traditions were still relevant and which were no longer so. At that meeting Oskar Brecher was sympathetic to this approach and to the goal of articulating a living Reform Judaism that meets the intellectual and spiritual needs of sophisticated Jews in the twenty-first century.

A few weeks later a small group of rabbis and laypeople were brought together to consider what should be done to right the balance back toward the Reform mainstream. At that meeting, I and Professor Lance J. Sussman of the University at Binghamton and rabbi of Temple Concord of Binghamton were asked to draw up a statement that could be offered to rabbis and congregational leaders as more representative of what Reform Judaism stood for than the inadequate CCAR document. The two us worked during that summer to formulate this draft. Because of circumstances beyond our control, the document was only circulated privately and not given wide distribution. Rabbi Sussman and I together wrote an article for the Journal of the Central Conference of American Rabbis explaining in detail why we felt the new Pittsburgh Platform was a turn in the wrong direction,[2] but the alternative platform we drafted has never appeared in

---

[2] Lance J. Sussman and Robert M. Seltzer, "Pittsburgh II and the Crisis of Confidence in the Reform Rabbinate," *CCAR Journal: A Reform*

WHAT ARE THE BASIC PRINCIPLES OF REFORM JUDAISM

print.

Because of Oskar Brecher's sympathetic concern for the survival of a Reform Judaism, we would like to take advantage of this publication in his honor to make available for the historical record our vision of the essentials of the movement at a crucial juncture in its history.

RMS

***

What Do We Really Believe?
The Enduring Principles of Reform Judaism

Introduction

The current discussion of a new platform for Reform Judaism is a window of opportunity for clarifying the movement's essential aims. A fresh interpretation of the relation of the movement to the Jewish tradition and to modernity is quite appropriate. The religious language and tone of Reform Judaism has shifted dramatically in the last half century, together with the social context and intellectual resources at its disposal. We hold that a platform should be an intellectually rigorous document reflective of the religious situation of the majority of Reform Jews and written in as simple language as possible. We feel that the basic epistemological presuppositions of the movement are still valid and that the forward-looking role that Reform has played in modern Judaism fulfills a vital need in the contemporary religion. There are certain broad principles which characterize the whole sweep of the Reform experience and connect our movement from the days of the pioneering synagogues of Seesen in Germany and Charleston in South Carolina to the present. A restatement of them should present Reform as a movement characterized by a conscious response to change as well as dedicated to the preservation of Judaism.

Unfortunately, in our opinion, the "Statement of Principles" adopted by the Central Conference of American Rabbis in Pittsburgh in May, 1999 attempts to reorient Reform Judaism in a direction at odds with many of today's best informed and most devoted Reform Jews and with the history of the movement. With the hope of offering Reform Jews a better grounded and more representative presentation of their religious convictions, we have prepared our own "Statement of Principles for Reform Judaism." It is our hope that this alternative formulation will help return the movement to its fundamental commitment as an open minded, flexible, consciously self-critical expression of an ancient faith.

In our view, a Reform statement of principles for the coming decade must go beyond the acknowledgment that an irreversible process of modernization has completely repositioned Judaism in both the public and private realms. Just as our predecessors reconsidered their Judaism as result of political emancipation, Reform Judaism should continue to acknowledge the implications of historical scholarship and the comparative study of religion, which have transformed our understanding of the nature of religion as such. Doing so is not measuring Judaism by an external and alien standard; it is a matter of courageous truthfulness in facing up to the intellectual breakthroughs of the modern world that have occurred since the Enlightenment. Modern historical consciousness requires that one always consider the setting and context of every classical work and phase of Judaism from the emergence of ancient Israel to the present. A viable Reform platform must also acknowledge the rational critique of Jewish belief that was a hallmark of Jewish philosophy in the past which has become fully self-conscious in Reform Judaism. To be sure, the concept of reason has gone through various formulations over time, but coherence, consistency, and universality remain central. Above all, a platform for our time should firmly reiterate the priority of ethics over ritual.

We are hardly advocating a return to the language of the first Pittsburgh Platform of 1885 with its blanket dismissal of many Jewish ceremonies and its overly optimistic view of progress. We appreciate the existential symbolism of ritual action and of some of the Jewish rituals our religious forebears abandoned in the quest for respectability. Reappropriation of these rituals is not a return to the past; it is creativity in the present. Indeed, these can be considered new rituals recast in the mold of old ones, linking ourselves with our origins. We do insist, however, that ritual is not an end in itself.

The formulators of the 1885 document had in mind a hierarchy of sacred responsibilities, a Jewish concept not present in the 1999 Pittsburgh statement. Historical Judaism since the prophets requires a hierarchy of Jewish duty. Any new platform should insist on the prophetic centrality of ethics in our understanding of Reform Judaism. Judaism's powerful ethical thrust as doing God's will constitutes the spiritual ground of our calling as a people and the most important reason for the Jews to continue in perpetuity as a community of faith.

Reform Judaism has always had its eye fixed on the future, not only on the past. In our view, Reform seeks to enrich the palette of Judaism and honors the human ability to re-think and re-feel tradition. It affirms the abiding centrality of God, Torah, and Israel. God is our deepest trust in the good. Torah is more than learning what has already been thought and said. The Jewish religion is more than an heirloom passed down to us from earlier centuries; it is a continuing creative synthesis, an unfinished tapestry constantly being woven as well as conserved. Israel represents the central role the Jews have played in the religious history of humankind.

The mandate of Reform Judaism is to be critical and creative, faithful to the highest visions of our prophets and sages and open to new knowledge. It would be very unfortunate if Reform Judaism were to define itself mainly in contrast to contemporary Orthodox Judaism, not as a position with an integrity of its own. To be effective and fulfilling as a religious movement we have to be confident that Reform Judaism represents as accurately as it can the abiding elements of Judaism in ways compelling to our generation. Reform Judaism believes that a profound faith in the teachings of Judaism can be united with a questioning temper. Reform draws on critical scholarship and encourages its flourishing as the intellectual mode of our movement, because it insists on a passion for truth, as well as justice and morality, as supreme Jewish values. Reform Judaism is far more profound and at peace with itself than conveyed by the new Pittsburgh Platform.

We have endeavored to articulate a short, cogent set of principles that we believe are appropriate for our time. The vision of Judaism that we tried to convey in this alternative statement seeks to be inclusive on an individual and communal level. We affirm the possibility of genuine faith in God in a scientific and technological dominated age and the constructive use of reason in an age marked by an inchoate spiritual quest. We affirm human freedom to do the right at a time when people believe in inexorable causes and in a view of the world that is compatible with the demanding achievements of science and philosophy when these offer confusing lessons. We affirm a loyalty to the ancient Jewish tradition in a time when reliance on the past is considered dubious, and an openness to on-going literary and artistic creativity when many yearn for traditional stability. Out of these negations come the affirmation that is Reform Judaism at its best.

Because the CCAR's 1999 Statement of Principles does not embrace our heartfelt view of Reform, we respectfully offer

WHAT ARE THE BASIC PRINCIPLES OF REFORM JUDAISM

a Statement of Principles broader in its appeal and embodying a philosophy of Judaism which is comprehensive and cogent. Through it we hope that "*hesed* and *emet* (lovingkindness and truth) embrace, *tzedek* and *shalom* (justice and peace) kiss" (Psalm 85:11).

A Statement of Principles for Reform Judaism as it Approaches its Third Century

The Reform movement emerged nearly two centuries ago in response to a series of unprecedented challenges to traditional Judaism. Its early adherents took the lead with daring measures to make our tradition accessible to modern Jews. They enriched the Jewish tradition through scholarship, theological writings, and innovations in the liturgy and in the synagogue. We believe that the basic tenets of the Reform movement, refined in the crucible of historical experience, are a model for a living, authentic Judaism today. In this spirit, we rededicate ourselves to the central principles of Reform Judaism for our time.

1. We hold that Judaism has always been capable of adapting to unforeseeable situations while preserving its core of symbols and ideals. Jewish history is a record of this adaptability and enduring faith. As Reform Jews, we are conservators of what we have inherited and responsible for a Jewish future that maintains its spiritual relevance. We believe that Reform Judaism has offered a satisfying mode of Jewish expression for innumerable Jews around the world. We affirm our fellowship with other expressions of Jewishness, seeking with them to sustain our Jewish heritage. We hold that the Reform movement has contributed to the vitality of Judaism by acting as a vanguard.

2. We affirm that Judaism offers a spiritual grounding in a cosmic order that evokes in us awe and mystery. We insist that morality is central to Judaism and that this cosmic order confers

ethical responsibilities on us as beings with the capacity to choose between good and evil. We are convinced that modern historical and scientific knowledge has far-reaching implications for our understanding of the universe, the evolution of religion, and the development of Judaism --and that this knowledge calls on us to reexamine our presuppositions in every generation.

3. We find sustenance of soul in Jewish memories, holy days, and prayers. They affirm our connection to the Jewish people, deepen our relation to God, and make us better human beings. Reform Jewish ritual and ceremony give our lives order and structure. In the weave of weekday and Shabbat, in the symbolism of the Jewish year, and in the cycle of a Jewish life we find ways to bring the sacred into our lives and to reach out to one another. We undertake to observe those traditional religious practices that enrich our human condition. Education and reflection may lead us to discontinue observances that run counter to our conscience, however useful these may have been in the past. We introduce new Jewish rituals that strengthen our moral resolve and add spiritual depth to our lives.

4. Even though our personal theologies may differ, we maintain that a meaningful, responsible life imbued with sensitive regard for others is rooted in faith in a transcendent source of being and goodness. Judaism offers hope and succor in the struggle with doubt, suffering, and death. Our religion provides ineffable moments of communion with God. It is the ground for affirming the exemplary power of morally courageous deeds, the sanctity of life, and the possibility of personal transcendence through apprehension of spiritual beauty. In face of the many forms of misery and evil around us, we assert our role as partners of God in repairing the world and furthering the continual work of redemption.

5. We affirm that the life-long study of Torah is a central Jewish duty and privilege. We recognize in the ongoing interpretation of Torah a developing and unfolding of ethical and spiri-

tual truths by our prophets, sages, and our teachers through the ages down to the present. Our broad view of Torah is compatible with reason, historical knowledge, scientific thought, and democratic values. We affirm the beauty and value of the Hebrew language in religious observance and in the learning of Torah.

 6. We acknowledge our own heartfelt ties to Jewish life in the Land of Israel where Judaism first arose, the return to which Jews have long dreamed of and have achieved in our lifetime. We view Zionism and the establishment of a Jewish state as an idealistic and creative expression of Jewish survival and renaissance in modern times. We encourage the growth of liberal and flexible forms of Judaism in Israel even as we affirm the Diaspora as a permanent feature of Jewish life with its own unique challenges and opportunities.

 7. We reject isolating ourselves as individuals or a group from the moral, social, and cultural concerns of the worlds in which we live. We view the plurality of traditions and peoples as legitimate expressions of human nature that will endure in the age of global interconnectedness that we have entered. In the spirit of the Jewish teaching that the righteous of all peoples merit salvation, we encourage undertakings with other faiths for the betterment of society and mutual appreciation of each tradition's highest ideals. We reach out in friendship to all those who share Jewish values. We welcome those who wish to become Jews and join our religious quest. Together we will endeavor to create Jewish homes, support Jewish philanthropic and cultural institutions, and ensure that our synagogues are fitting places of worship, study, and moral action.

 8. Standing firmly in the modern world, we appreciate deeply the insights embodied in a heritage that has endured for more than 3,000 years. We interpret the traditional view of the uniqueness of the Jewish people as an affirmation of Judaism's central role in the spiritual history of humanity. As enunciated

by the biblical prophets and explained in classical Jewish writings, this aspiration stands for the Jewish mission to represent the highest moral and religious values. We recommit ourselves to the ideals of truthfulness, justice, compassion, and universal peace as envisioned by the prophets -- humanity's best hope in the new age it has entered.

Robert M. Seltzer was ordained by the Hebrew Union College – Jewish Institute of Religion in 1961. He is Professor of History and Jewish Studies at Hunter College of the City University of New York, and a member of Temple Israel.
Lance J. Sussman was in the 1980 ordination class of the Hebron Union College-Jewish Institute of Religion. He was recently appointed as senior rabbi of Reform Congregation Keneseth Israel in Elkins Park, Pennsylvania.

THE SQUARE ROOT OF 10,000
Or
WHEN IS 100 NOT 100?

Leonard Kravitz

I begin with the statement of a profound thinker who, while not noted as a technical philosopher, still has provided us with a number of insights into various philosophical problems. The thinker to whom I refer is Peanuts and the statement to which I advert is his insightful remark that "There is no problem so big that we can't run away from it."

The problem, which I suggest, required running from is that of affect in God. That problem touches much of medieval Jewish (and Christian and Islamic) philosophy. It may move the thinker to flight because it sets in opposition the two competing systems of texts, the two contrasting elements of thought of the medieval theological synthesis, the particular religious tradition and the particular philosophical tradition which served as the matrix for the synthesis. According to the various religious traditions (and here we might focus on the Jewish religious tradition) God is pleased, angry, and sad; He loves and He hates. With compassion, He hears the prayers of His people when they are in difficulty and in His love He has given them His law for their benefit. In sum, He is affected by His creatures, even as He wishes to affect them. The notion of covenant is correlative with the notion of Divine Affect.

According to the philosophical tradition, God is beyond affect; He is too exalted to enter into relation with His creatures.

For the philosophers, affect is a diminishing of the nature of deity; for them were God affected, He would not be God. As the philosopher who appears in the opening pages of the Kuzari puts it,

> "There is no favor or dislike in (the nature of) God, because He is above desire and intention. A desire intimates a want in the person who feels it, and not till is it satisfied does he become (so to speak) complete. If it remains unfulfilled, he lacks completion." (*Kuzari* I: 1, Hirshfeld translation, pp 31,32)

An incomplete deity would lack the requisite perfection of the philosopher's concept of God. More than that: for the philosopher, even a Jewish philosopher such as Saadia Gaon, the notion of affect carries with it the notion of corporeality--- even though that may not be apparent at first glance. As Saadia put it,

> "As for those who do not seek to affirm that God is a body yet insist on arrogating for Him motion or rest or anger or good will or the like, they really arrogate for Him a corporeal character by way of implication, even if they do not do it expressly. They act like the individual who says, "I do not demand of Reuben one hundred drachmas, but I demand of him the square root of 10,000." (B/O, II: Exordium, Rosenblatt translation, p 93)

If anger or good will entails the notion of corporeality, what are we to do with a tradition replete with such expressions related to God? We seem forced on the horns of a dilemma: accept favor or disfavor in God and accept corporeality and indeed anthropomorphism; accept the incorporeality of Deity and reject favor and disfavor in God--- and with that rejection, reject much of the internal logic of the Tradition of God's favor in the past, His love for His people Israel which He manifested in selecting them to receive His Torah and the request for

God's favor which Jews asked for as they recited the words of the Amidah's paragraph, *Retzeh b'amcha Israel* -- asking God's favor in the present.

A possible solution to the dilemma would be to suggest that the words of the Tradition did not mean what they seemed to mean, that somehow, one could garner the square root of 10,000 all the while denying that he was receiving the 100. Thus Saadia would argue that the problem rests in God language, which by its nature was imprecise:

> "Were we, in our effort to give an account of God, to make use only of expressions that are literally true, it would be necessary for us to desist from speaking of Him as one who hears and sees and pities and wills to the point where there would be nothing left for us to affirm except the fact of His existence." (Saadia, B/O, II:8,P 118)

Again a dilemma: to say that God wills and pities is, as Saadia himself has said is to "…really arrogate for Him a corporeal character by way of implication"(B/O II: Ex, p 93); to merely affirm the fact of the Divine Existence would not support "the lofty, exalted ideas" suggested by these anthropopathic expressions (B/O II: 9,P 115) nor the law upon which they are seemingly based.

A possible solution used by Saadia, which will be followed by some of his successors, is to make terms such as pleasure or anger with reference to God to refer instead to outcomes with reference to men. Thus Saadia will tell his reader that whenever Scripture would have God say

> "… that He is pleased or angry, what is meant thereby is that whenever happiness and reward are decreed for some of God's creatures, that is characterized as God's pleasure… (W)hen some of them are deserving of hard-

ship and punishment, that is characterized as God's anger." (B/O II:11, p 123)

Thus the pleasure of God or the anger of God become metaphors for aspects of the human condition: to be happy is to know God's pleasure; to suffer is to know God's anger. Thus God has been delivered from the problem of affect by putting differing (though valid) interpretations on man's feeling.

How could the most positive human feeling encompass God's love in the Giving of the Torah? How could a God without affect give a Law, which seemingly would invite pleasure in its performance and anger in its nonperformance? I suggest that Saadia's approach was among the first to bridge the gap between the notion of a God beyond affect and of a Law which was His product: if the Law were that which would fit into the human condition, indeed were most expressive of the human condition, then God could be both its source and its unaffected transmitter. As God was the source of that which made human beings human, He could be the source of that which responded to that humanity. In sum God was reason and His Torah was reason. If on the one hand, we remember the opening lines of the *Book of Beliefs and Opinions*:

> "Blessed be God, the God of Israel, Who alone is deserving of being regarded as the Evident Truth, Who verifies with certainty unto rational beings the existence of their souls, by means of which they assess accurately the objects of their knowledge" (B/O Intro Treatise, p 3)

and on the other hand reflect on his opening statement in the Third Treatise dealing with Command and Prohibition that

> "... logic demands that whoever does some thing good be compensate either by means of a favor shown to him, if he is in need of it, or by means of thanks, if he does not require any regard...It was...necessary for Him to com-

mand His creatures to serve Him and thank Him for having created them. Reason also demands that he that is wise do not permit himself to be treated with contempt or to be insulted. It was, therefore, necessary for the Creator to forbid His servants to conduct themselves in such a way toward Him. Furthermore, reason demands that the creatures be prevented from wronging each other in all sorts of ways. Hence it was also necessary for the All-Wise not to permit them to do such a thing. Reason also deems it proper for a wise man to give employment to an individual who performs a certain function and to pay him a wage for it, merely in order to confer a benefit upon him, since this is something that redounds to the benefit of the worker without hurting the employer.
If, now, we were to combine these four classes of requirements, their sum-total would make up all the laws prescribed for us by our Lord.
(B/O, III: 1,p 139)

We understand the rational nature of the law: the entire Torah is the product of reason growing out of the initial act of the kindness of God in conferring being upon His creatures. (B/O III: Ex.p 137) If the Torah be in principle that which is given by reason and reducible to reason: viz., i.e., to serve God and not to offend Him, to help one's fellowman and not to hurt him, then the production of the Torah on the part of God need not be due to love beyond the initial act of creating the world nor its apprehension of our part need not be due to our responding in love beyond our pursuit of that Evident Truth which is God.

The pursuit of truth, alas, takes time. Even if one were to fit, as does Saadia the four aforementioned categories into the divisions of rational and revealed (B/O III: 1, p 140) we would still be faced with the difficulties of insuring their observance by the generality of people. Hence Saadia sees the necessity of prophets not only for the revealed but for the rational *mitzvot* as well. (B/O III: 3 p 145) Prophets were required for definitions of status, for definitions of property, and for definitions of punishment, so that one would know what precisely constituted fornication and what marriage, what was property, and therefore what was stealing, and what were the meet penalties for the transgressions of specific laws. (B/O III: 8,p 146) In sum: prophets were necessary for the establishment of the particular boundaries of society.

The individual could be rewarded or punished, not because he pleased or angered God but because he did what was unreasonable or anti-social. As Saadia would say with regard to God's hating,

> "Our Lord...does not hate anything on account of His own personality, because it is impossible that He be affected by any of the accidents appertaining to mortals. He considers them objectionable, only on our account, because of the harm they might afflict upon us. For if we transgress against Him, by failing to acknowledge our indebtness to Him, we are guilty of folly. On the other hand, if we wrong one another, we bring about the destruction of our lives and our wealth." (B/O IV: 4, p 190)

Thus ingratitude to God is folly and violence toward another is self-destruction. It would seem that Saadia avoided the 100 drachmas of God's pleasure and/or anger and the square root of 10,000 of God's affect. And yet his book, the *Book of Beliefs and Opinions* is replete with verses from Torah and statements from the Rabbis which describe God acting and being affected. For him, God was more than mere existence, than being described as He is... and yet Saadia's struggle with the dilemma of language affirming and yet denying affect in God would remain an ongoing problem.

To the reader who runs, it would seem that there would be no problem of affect in the thinking of Halevi. Yet a close reading of the Kuzari reveals that for him as for others, affect in God presented as much of a problem as it had for the philosopher who appeared in the beginning of the book. That philosopher we had heard at the beginning of Part One; he was echoed at the beginning of Part Two when the Rabbi (the Rabbi!) instructing the king of the Khazars tells him that

> "All names of God, save the Tetragrammaton, are predicates and attributive descriptions, derived from the way His creatures are affected by His decrees and measures. He is called merciful, if He improves the condition of any man whom people pity for his sorry plight. They attribute to Him mercy and compassion, although this is… surely nothing but a weakness of the soul… This cannot be applied to God, who is a just judge ordaining the poverty of one individual and the wealth of another. His nature remains quite unaffected by it." (Kuzari II: 2, p 73)

How can unaffected God, for Whom pity would be "a weakness of the soul," reveal His law to a particular people? For the philosopher appearing in the Kuzari and for many philosophers of the Middle Ages, such revelation would be impossible. Yet in a strange way that philosopher provides a clue to the means by which Halevi might join an affectless God with a specific revelation. Halevi has the philosopher speak of the Active Intellect, the means by which he and other philosophers attain the truth, activate their own intellects, attain perduration, and indeed reach

> "…what is called allusively and approximately Pleasure of God." (*Kusari* I: 1, p 33)

For the philosopher, (as we shall hear in more detail), from Maimonides (*Guide* II:18, Pp299ff)) the Active Intellect is unchanging. Its effect is dependent on the level of preparation of the would be philosopher, not on a change in the affect of the Deity.

What the philosopher will call the Active Intellect, Halevi will call the Divine Influence (the Inyan Elohi in Ibn Tibbon's translation) (Kuzari V: 10,P 228) It too is unchanging: As Halevi puts it,

> "The Divine Influence is beneficent and desirous of doing good to all. Wherever something is arranged and prepared to receive His guidance; He does not refuse it, nor withhold it, nor hesitate to shed light, wisdom, and inspiration on it. If, however, the order is disturbed, it cannot receive this light, which is, then lost. The Divine Influence is above change or damage." (Kuzari II: Pp 89)

If for the philosopher, the Active Intellect were beyond change, then variety of outcomes of conjunction with it would be due to the variety of the intellects coming, as it were, into contact with it. One might wonder, how for Halevi could an unchanging Divine Influence produce a specific outcome, the Torah, to the Jewish People? This specific outcome could occur if the Jewish People was different from all others! Now we understand Halevi's statements that we Jews "are cream of mankind"(Kuz. I: 27,p 41,) that "Israel among the nations is like the heart amidst the organs of the body" (Kuz.II36,p 95) and that

> "The sons of Jacob were...distinguished from other people by godly qualities, which made them, so to speak an angelic caste." (Kuz. I: 103, P 64)

As all animals are not rational and hence are unable to take advantage of rationality, so all men are not Jews and hence are unable to take advantage of the Divine Influence. There is a qualitative difference between animals and men. So there is a qualitative difference between men and those able to connect into that Divine Influence, namely Jews! They can receive the benefits of the Torah produced by the combination of the Divine influence, the right place, Palestine, (Kuzari II: 12,p 78) and the right language, Hebrew (II: 68, p 109). Thus Halevi can logically have the Rabbi tell the Khazar king that

> "We still hold connection with that Divine Influence through the laws which He has placed as a link between us and Him." (Kuz. II: 33,p 94)

This is not to say that there is not an internal stratification in the sense of ranks among those who are in conjunction with the Divine Influence, even as there are ranks among those who think that they are in conjunction with the Active Intellect. Conjunction requires self-control (Kuz. V: 10, p 228) and a soul susceptible to the intellect. (Kuz. II:26, p 90); but such conjunction in principle is available only in the line of Adam and Abraham and Abraham's descendants. (Kuz. I: 95, p 58)

Thus Halevi has solved the problem of affect in God by fixing on the genetic aspect of some men.

Bahya Ibn Pakuda, whose dates are uncertain (c. 1080 – 1156) and whose *Duties of the Heart* was the most popular moral-religious book in all Jewish literature, would seem to be one who would be far from the problem of affect. Yet his treatment of affect in God stands close to much of Saadia and anticipates much that will be found in Maimonides.

The first section of his book deals with the Unity of God which he who would fulfill the Duties of the Heart must first learn. There are four stages: the first to know the words dealing with the unity of God--- simply to use the words. The second stage is the attainment of the truth with the mind as well as with the mouth. It is to follow the tradition, like being in a company of blind men, each with his hand on the shoulder of the one ahead of him, so that finally one with sight may lead the entire band. The third stage is the acknowledgement of the Creator's unity in words and in thought according, as he puts it,

"...to the method of rational investigation, without the knowledge however, of what is implied by the true unity as distinguished from conventional unity.." (DOH, translated by Moses Hyamson, Treatise One, Gate of Unity, Chapter II, pp 63,65)

The fourth stage is

"... the acknowledgement of the Unity of God with mind and speech, after one knows how to adduce proofs of His existence and has arrived at a knowledge of the truth of His unity by the method of rational investigation and by arguments that are right and reasonable. (P 65)

Rational investigation and arguments that are right and reasonable suggest a philosophical orientation somewhat surprising for an ethical tractate. Yet they are crucial in understanding Bahya's approach to the problem of affect. He discusses the attributes ascribed to God; his discussion operates on two planes; what the attributes really mean and why they are used. The language in which they are framed is not to be taken literally but nonetheless has a purpose, as Bahya tells his reader,

"Whatever attributes you ascribe to the Creator, you are to infer from them the denial of their contraries. As Aristotle said, 'Negatives give a truer conception of God's attributes than affirmatives' ...The active attributes of the Deity are those ascribed to the Creator with reference to His works...<u>We are permitted, however, to ascribe these qualities to Him, because of the urgent need of acquainting ourselves with and realizing his existence, so that we may assume the obligation of his service.</u>" (DOH, Unity of God, Chapter X, Hyamson p 103) (underlining mine)

The use of attributes and the ascription of affect come out of human need not out of Divine reality. Bahya continues

> "First, attributes are ascribed... as indicate form and bodily likeness... Second, attributes are ascribed connoting bodily movements and actions, as in, 'And the Lord smelt' (Gen. 8:21) 'And the Lord saw' (Gen: 6:5)... 'And it grieved the Lord in His heart' (Gen: 6:6)...What we are all agreed upon is that necessity forced us to ascribe corporeal attributes to God and to describe Him by attributes properly belonging to His creatures, <u>so as to obtain some conception by which the thought of God's existence should be fixed in the minds of men</u>" (DOH, Unity, X H p 105) (underlining mine)

Like Saadia, Bahya holds that the necessity for attributes of and affect in God arise out of the difficulties of language and human incapacity, for he tells us that

> "...had they (the prophets) limited themselves to more abstract terms and concepts appropriate to God, <u>we would have understood neither the terms nor the concepts</u>" (DOH, Unity, X, p 107) (underlining mine)

That lack of understanding would have had its resultant:

> "And it would have been impossible for us to worship a being whom we did not know, since the worship of the unknown is impossible." (ibid)

We have again the square root of 10,000 and 100. To worship we must know, but the terms we use to provide knowledge we know do not describe that which we could, worship! Indeed a paradox!

Bahya tells his reader that he must start slowly with the worshipper and "deal discreetly with him" and strive to make him understand that the presentation in the Tradition of the image of God is but "approximate and metaphorical." In truth, on reflection, one must conclude that it is less than metaphorical, the language which employs attribute and affect is without content. It is necessitated, alas, by mankind being divided into two distinct groups, those who can understand, and by <u>understand,</u> we mean <u>philosophically</u> understand, and those who cannot understand. As Bahya continues,

> "The wise thinker will endeavor to strip the husk of the terms, their materialistic meaning from the kernel and will raise his conception step by step, till he at last will attain as much of the knowledge of the truth as his intellect is capable of apprehending...Had Scripture, when expounding this theme, employed a terminology appropriate in its exactness but only intelligible to the profound thinker, <u>the majority of mankind, because of their intellectual deficiency and weak perception in things spiritual, would have been left without a religion.</u>" (DOH, p 107) (underlining mine)

And further:

> "<u>But the word which may be understood in a material sense will not hurt the intelligent person, since he recognizes its real meaning and it will help the simple, as its use will result in fixing in his heart and mind the conception that he has a creator whom he is bound to serve.</u>"(DOH, p107) (underlining mine)

One wonders about those simple folk, the 'majority of mankind" and the religion which is theirs. Will they ever know the truth and thus achieve that understanding of the Unity of God which stands at the beginning of the Duties of the Heart? Are they to continue to worship that which they cannot know? Is the notion of affect in God which the philosopher knows to be false, necessary for the simple folk that they may serve their Creator by following His law?

Does the term 'the majority of mankind' encompass the non-Jews as well? Are their Scriptures equivalent to ours, a question which an Averroes could easily answer but which

THE SQUARE ROOT OF 10,000 OR WHEN IS 100 NOT 100?

seems strange to put to the writer of the Duties of the Heart. Has Bahya followed the instruction of the philosopher of the Kuzari to choose a religion for the management of the household and the country?

Even if we turn to Torah, what is its meaning? Bahya provides us with a parable of the guest of a wealthy man who arrived at his host's establishment with his flocks and his herds. The host provided much barley for the cattle, but only enough food for the man. So, Bahya explains,

> "So, too the Hebrew language as well as the books of the prophets and the writings of the pious, when referring to the attributes of the Creator make liberal use of the concrete expressions ...which are such as people easily understand and employ in their current vocabulary." (DOH, p 107)

The parallel between the masses and cattle and their inability to understand is suggested by Bahya in yet another statement:

> "A philosopher once said: he whose mind is incapable of grasping the abstract, fastens on the terms used in Divinely given Scriptures, and is unaware that the style of the Biblical books is adapted to the intelligence of those to whom they were addressed, but does not express the real nature of Him who addressed them and concerning Whom the terms are used. It is like the whistling call, when cattle are to be watered, which is more effective in making in the beast drink than clear and intelligent speech would be." (DOH, p119) (underlining mine)

And now having established that the words of Scripture are as whistles to gather in cattle, that the words themselves convey little or no content, Bahya proceeds in the very next section of the Duties of the Heart in the section called Trust, to tell the reader that trust is required when in any human situation, one feels the qualities of mercy, pity, and compassion Thus,

> "...when one knows that his neighbor feels pity and compassion for him, he will trust that person. His mind will be tranquil in matter with which he troubles the latter." (DOH, p 297)

Bahya then determines that there are in all seven conditions that make for trust, all of which we would describe as affects, and then says,

> "When we investigate these seven conditions, we will find none of them in any created creature, but all of them in the exalted creator. He is merciful to all His creatures, as it is said, "Merciful and Gracious is the Lord" (Ps. 103:8)

Thus we should trust because God cares; His care is revealed in the words of Scripture---and yet if we investigated those words, we might find that they "whistle." Once again we have the square root of 10,000 and the 100.

There was another writer who characterized the masses as animals, domestic or wild depending on their usefulness or their danger (MN II: 36, Pp 372) I refer of course to Maimonides who had a lot to say about the notion of affect. For him, the belief in affect was equivalent to the belief in idolatry. Indeed it was worse: if idolatry could be said to provoke God,

> "What should be the state of him whose infidelity bears upon His essence, may He be exalted, and consists in believing Him to be different from what He really is? I mean to say that he does not believe that He exists; or believes that there are two gods, or that He is a body, or that He is subject to affections; or again he ascribes to God some deficiency or other. Such a man is indubitably more blameworthy than a worshipper of idols... know accordingly; you who are that man, that when you believe in the corporeality of God or believe that one of the states of the body belongs to Him, you provoke His jealousy and an-

ger…and are a hater, an enemy, and an adversary of God, much more than an idolator." (MN: I:36, Pp84)

Yet the belief in affect in God might serve a purpose: Maimonides spoke of two kinds of beliefs, the one which was true and the other which was necessary, necessary for the sake of political welfare:

> "Such, for instance, is our belief that He, may He be exalted, is violently angry with those who disobey Him and that it is therefore necessary to fear Him and to dread Him and to take care not to disobey." (MN:III: 28, Pp511)

Not only is the affect of anger a necessary belief, but so too is the affect of pity, for Maimonides characterizes as necessary

> "…the belief that He, may He be exalted, responds instantaneously to the prayer of someone wronged or deceived: "and it shall come to pass, when he crieth out to me, that I will hear, for I am gracious." (Ex. 22:23) (III: 28, Pp514) (underline mine)

God's affective nature plays a role in the last chapter of the Guide, which many have thought to be Maimonides' reversal of his position and his acceptance of the notion that God may act in moral and indeed in affective way. The last chapter of the Guide is an extended Midrash on Jeremiah (9:22,23). Maimonides noted that had the verse ended merely to suggest the apprehension of God, it would have said,

> "But let him that glorieth glory in this, that he understands and knows Me; and would have stopped there; or he would have said: 'that he understandeth and know that I am One'…But he says that one should glory in the apprehension of Myself and in the knowledge of My attrib-

utes, by which he meant My actions, as we made clear with reference to the dictum: SHOW ME NOW THY WAYS and so on. In this verse, he made clear to us that those actions that ought to be known and imitated are LOVING KINDNESS, JUDGMENT, AND RIGHTEOUSNESS. He adds another corroborative notion through saying in the earth--- this being the pivot of the Law." (*Guide* III: 54, Pp637)

The adept reader will remember that Maimonides in an earlier chapter had established the notion that THE WAYS of God and the Characteristics, the *Midot*, were identical and hence were attributes of action which really did not describe God but whose emulation might be useful:

"Those actions are needed for the governance of cities" (*Guide* I: 54, Pp128)

Since these are attributes, one learns to negate them. Indeed, one comes closer to God with every negation. Indeed, the more negations of Divine attribute, the more perfection for the human thinker.

"… in every case in which the demonstration that a certain thing should be negated with reference to Him becomes clear to you, you become more perfect." (Guide I: 59 Pp, 139)

The terms: loving-kindness, judgment, and righteousness in the quotation of Jeremiah in III: 54, must be understood in light of three words *Hasid, Zadik, Shofet*, the verbal forms the words in chapter previous III:53. As Maimonides interprets them, none of them have a moral content. God is "..called *Hasid* because He brought the all into being; as *Zadik* because of His mercy to the weak---I refer to the governance of the living being by means of its forces; and as Judge (*Shofet*) because of occurrence in the world of relative good things and relative great calamities, necessitated by judgment that is consequent wisdom" (*Guide* III:53, Pp 632---the adept will understand what is meant by judgment consequent on unchanging wisdom.)

Asher ba'aretz, "in the earth"—is the instruction to the reader of the Guide that the terms suggesting affect teach the would-be philosopher to engage in the continual negation of terms applied to the deity all the while using those terms for the governance of cities, for here on this earth, one has to deal the multitude who inhabit this earth.

Mere reflection on Maimonides' theory of prophecy as the resultant of the action of the Active Intellect upon the rational and imaginative faculties should make it clear that no affect is required of the Deity to dispense an ever flowing and eternal influence. If one remembered Maimonides' words that his view of prophecy differed from that of the philosopher in that he held that God could withhold prophecy, in a manner like unto other miracles, he should wonder in what way could God stop the ever active Active Intellect, an immaterial being, which like God is ever in actu?

In Maimonides' system, then, the notion of affect in God is a whip to smite the philosophically unprepared; it has its uses as a necessary political device, but it is empty of meaning. It will guarantee prayer and we here might contrast III: 32 and III:44, prayer like sacrifice in its time is a matter of custom --- and the Shema and the Tefillah are "necessary" and they bring about "useful opinions." (*Guide* III:44,Pp 574)

In Albo, if the pun can be forgiven, one has a *col-bo* of Jewish philosophical thinking, since his *Ikkarim* is an eclectic summary of the parade of previous Jewish thinkers. Albo, as might be expected, treats affect in God, in much the same way as his predecessors. The notion of God as immaterial being precludes affect; thus Albo says,

> "It has already been proved demonstratively that God is neither a body nor a force residing in a body. It follows

that we must deny God all bodily accident and corporeal affections. "(*Ikkarim* II: 14, p 81)

Even so, the belief in affect in God serves a useful and indeed 'necessary' purpose in the affairs of men:

> "The purpose of the prophets is to lead all mankind to worship God and to love Him. But the masses of the people cannot be made to humble themselves for service except from fear of punishment. Now since, in human phraseology, when a king punishes those who rebelled...he is said to be jealous and revengeful and full of wrath, so the prophets say God... that He is a jealous and avenging God and is full of wrath..." (*Ikkarim* II:14, P 82)

As wrath and anger really do not relate to God, neither does joy, for

> "... joy is the perception of the agreeableness of a pleasant and appropriate thing. It is without doubt an affection." (*Ikkarim* II:15, p 90)

Strangely enough, in the manner of the square root of 10,000 and the 100, God and a certain kind of person can have joy, for

> "...the joy of God in His own essence is unlimited and continuous, because every kind of perfection that He appreciates in Himself is infinite, and in His essence are contained an infinite number of perfections...
> And yet by divine grace a person may comprehend a certain degree of their excellence, a point referred to...(by) 'How precious is thy loving kindness O God! And the children of men take refuge in the shadow of Thy wings.' (Ps 36:8)... The meaning therefore is that which is infinite can not be attained, but remains hidden and concealed, yet men take refuge in that hidden shadow, containing the mystery of God's essence...The Psalmist also

says that by reason of the understanding they acquire of that mystery, the understanding, namely, that all existing things emanate from Him by a chain of causation…they derive wonderful pleasure and satisfaction in the spiritual world." (*Ikkarim* II: 15, pp 94,95)

So God and the one who can contemplate the great chain of being can both have joy, a joy it should be noted that is restricted to philosophers whether Divine or human.

One might wonder whether such a joy would lead to God choosing or willing. Here we will come to Albo's theory of divine attributes. As many of those who preceeded him, Albo had a two-fold system of attributes. The first deals with God as necessary existent and the second deals with our understanding of perfection. What is interesting is that Albo puts will into the first category, saying

"…Such attributes are one, eternal, perpetual, wise, having will…" (*Ikkarim* II: 21, p 124)

It is clear that Albo is following Maimonides' argument that the Divine Will, the Divine Wisdom, and the Divine Essence are all one and the same. (*Guide* MN II: 18, Pp 302) Thus if God be one, eternal, and perpetual, then 'having will' is the same as the aforementioned other three. The Divine Will is unchanging. It is only by analogy to human acts, that we can say that God desires or wills, for

"…since we see acts emanating from God which are similar to those acts which emanate from a voluntary agent, we speak of God as desiring and willing; though we cannot understand how will and desire reside in God without causing change and affection. This is unknown to us as the nature of His knowledge is unknown to us." (*Ikkarim* II: 24, P 145)

Thus Albo escapes the dilemma of God's desiring and thus being affected or God's not desiring and thus operating by necessity, by pleading ignorance. So Albo, too, would like the square root of 10,000 of God's desire and will without the 100 of God's being affected.

Perhaps Albo's following of Maimonides' view of attributes in general even to using Maimonides' proof-text may sum up the argument:

> "In reality, however, it is impossible to ascribe any attribute to Him, even one which is based on His acts, in the manner which we ascribe it to a human being...The most fitting praise is silence, as David says, 'For thee, silence is praise.' (Ps 65:4)" (*Ikkarim* II: 23, Pp 141)

Silence may be the best prescription in speaking of affect in God. Yet Albo, like all who went before him, spoke and did not keep silent. What he meant remains problematic.

What shall we make of this admittedly spotty survey of medieval Jewish Philosophy and its relation to affect in God? It would seem that on one level, affect became the measure of the philosophical acuity of the thinker; the more affect in God, the less the ability and training of the thinker; the less affect in God, the more the thinker has absorbed the teachings of philosophy.

The more affect in God, the more that the law is safeguarded for the person bereft of philosophical training; the more the philosophical training, the less the need for affect in God, in as much as the would be philosopher, by passing through his training regimen has already controlled the passions which would have him break the law and thus require the threats and promises that an affective God could provide.

There seems to be another linkage: the more that God is thought to have affect: to choose and to love, the less 'rational' the Law, which He will provide, will be. The less affect in the Deity, the more rational the law will be. The more affect, the more particularity; the less affect, the less particularity (and if one could say it, the more universalism) thus, that even a Bahya speaks about the majority of mankind suggests a community of interest with some one like Al Farabi (in his Plato) or someone who came later, like Averroes.

What seems clear is that the issue of affect was not directly faced; at times, it seemed that the thinkers wished both to affirm and to deny it--- as if to keep the square root of 10,000 and yet give away the 100 drachmas.

We have then a two-fold system of understanding Scripture: affect is the key: society is maintained by a theory of God, which the mass-man accepts and the elite philosopher rejects. Affect then is symbolic of the two levels of society, the elite and the masses joined together by words and divided by meanings. The philosophers (the elite) will understand those words in a way which the masses will not, indeed were the masses to have understood the words the way that the elite did, it would affect the position of the elite even as it would affect the society of which they were the ruling part. Hence, the notion of concealment found so often in medieval literature grows out of the two-fold nature of society, and the supposed two-fold nature of scripture. Affect then can stand as the symbol of that double separation: because the masses believe in God as a person, they believe in affect; because the elite believe in God as an idea, they don't believe in affect.

Thus two different groups understand the words of the Torah (and indeed, the entire Tradition) in totally different ways --- and indeed that was a problem, but it was a problem that people could run away from.

Bibliography

1. Saadia Gaon, *The Book of Beliefs and Opinions*, translated

from the Arabic and the Hebrew by Samuel Rosenblatt, New Haven, Yale University Press, 1948.

2. *The Book of Kuzari* by Judah Hallevi, translated from the Arabic by Hartwig Hirschfeld, New York, Pardes Publishing House, Inc. 1946.

3. *Duties of the Heart by Bachya ben Joseph ibn Paquda*, translated from the Arabic into Hebrew by Jehudah Ibn Tibbon with English translation by Moses Hyamson, Jerusalem, Boys Town Publishers, 1962.

4. *The Guide of the Perplexed by Moses Maimonides*, translated with an Introduction and Notes by Sholomo Pines, Chicago, University of Chicago Press, 1963, Second Impression 1969.

5. Sefer Ha-Ikkarim, *The Book of Principles by Joseph Albo*, Critically Edited on the Basis of Manuscripts and Old Editions and Provided with a Translation and Notes by Issac Husik, Philadelphis, The Jewish Publication Society of America, 1946

Leonard S. Kravitz was ordained by HUC-JIR in 1954. He is Professor of Midrash at the Hebrew Union College – Jewish Institute of Religion.

INTERPRETING THE AKEDAH YEAR BY YEAR

Robert M. Seltzer

Genesis 22, called the *Binding of Isaac* (*Akedat Yitzhak*), is certainly one of the most dramatic and puzzling chapters of the Torah. Why would God ask Abraham to sacrifice his child? Is God a capricious being who changes his mind? Why would Abraham agree to offer his beloved son without protest? Is Abraham's faith so great that it can lead to murder? And why should this very story be read at the morning service of Rosh ha-Shanah? (Actually, it is the Torah portion for Rosh ha-Shanah in Reform synagogues, whereas traditionally Genesis 21, the birth of Isaac, is read on the first day and Genesis 22 is read on the second day of the holiday. Hearing of Isaac's birth first, followed by the story of how he was almost killed by his own father, may even heighten the poignancy of the tale.)

The easy -- and wrong -- answer is to dismiss the tale as barbaric, as one of my students once insisted. Scholars such as Eric Auerbach in *Mimesis*, a classic study of the depiction of reality in literature, have called attention to the highly refined nature of the narrative where each detail, indeed each word, adds to the tension. Perhaps Genesis 22 is subtle in style but primitive in content and therefore should be replaced for the Jewish New Year Day by something more elevated? That is what Reform Judaism did for the Yom Kippur Torah reading, where passages from Deuteronomy 29 and 30 (*Netsavim*) were substituted for the description of the sacrificial offerings for the day as described in Leviticus 16. On the contrary: as time as described in Leviticus 16. On the contrary: as time passes, I realize the profound suggestiveness of the Akedah.

For 35 years I been given the honor of introducing the Torah readings for the high holydays. Three and a half decades of interpreting the Akedah? Wouldn't I have long ago run out of a new slant? Not at all. The story has turned out to be remarkably open to the discovery of hidden connections, subtly pregnant with new interpretative possibilities. Could this be one of the essential features of a writing that a religious tradition calls "revealed?" After all, no one reads the Epic of Gilgamesh, the Iliad and the Odyssey, Beowulf, or the Song of Roland regularly in worship services, however great these works are. In contrast, the Bible seems to have a way of being able to speak freshly to every new generation.

There have been several Judaisms in history -- biblical, Hellenistic, apocalyptic, rabbinic, philosophical, mystical, Enlightenment, Zionist, socialist. The modern Judaism of our time is yet another in this chain of synthesizing the tradition with different ages and cultural milieus. Over the years of delivering these Torah introductions I have tried to contribute to the recapturing of the lessons of the Akedah for liberal Jews at the end of the twentieth century. The following are several of my *divrei Torah* delivered to those who have come together to worship at the beginning of a season devoted to repentance and the resolve to become better persons.

1. The Divine Command

In our Torah portion this morning, chapter 22 of Genesis, the story of the binding of Isaac, we note that Abraham accepted without hesitation or demur that the voice he heard commanding him to sacrifice his son was indeed a divine voice. Why did he not question a directive from the very God who had promised that from Abraham would arise a people through whom all the nations of the earth will be blessed? The Torah portion also poses a second, even more difficult question: how could God have issued such a terrifying order to his beloved Abraham? We are told that it was a test -- but what kind of test could it possibly have been?

The first question may be the easier to answer. Living when Abraham did, there was no reason to doubt that such a command could come from a divinity. Child sacrifice was practiced in almost every ancient civilization across the globe. Everywhere priests officiated in ceremonies in which one offered valuable gifts to gods; child sacrifice was the most precious commodity of all -- the ultimate gift.

Perhaps eight or nine centuries after the time of Abraham and at least a century after Moses, we read in chapter 11 of Judges of an Israelite military hero, Jephthah, who vowed to sacrifice whatever came out of his door to meet him if he would return in safety from combat with the Ammonite foe. To his shock, what came out was his beloved daughter, his only child. Even Jephthah's daughter agreed that he had no choice but to fulfill the vow. The chapter poignantly concludes, "It became a custom that the daughters of Israel went year by year to lament the daughter of Jephthah the Gileadite four days in the year."

In 2 Kings 3:23-27 we read that Mesha, king of Moab, three centuries after Jephthah, found himself losing a war to the king of Israel, so he offered his first-born son as a burnt offering. The text relates, "There came great wrath upon Israel; and they withdrew from him and returned to their own land." Apparently Mesha's sacrifice had the intended effect, saving Moab from conquest.

In the late 600s BCE, two centuries after the war with Moab, the prophet Micah asked:

> With what shall I come before the Lord and
> bow myself before God on high?
> Shall I come before him with burnt offerings,

with calves a year old?
> Will the Lord be pleased with thousands of rams, with ten thousands of rivers of oil?
> Shall I give my first-born for my transgression, the fruit of my body for the sin of my soul?

The answer is a verse which has become justly famous as the epitome of biblical morality:

> He has showed you, O man, what is good; and what does the Lord require of you but to do justice, and to love kindness, and to walk humbly with your God. (Micah 6:6-8)

Apparently it was still credible to Micah's listeners that a divinity might require sacrificing one's child if circumstances were sufficiently dire.

Abraham did not protest God's command as outrageous or dismiss it as a thought implanted by a demon, because it was well within the expectations of someone living in ancient Canaan that even the most benevolent divine force might for unexplained reasons issue such a command.

What would Abraham have most likely felt when he heard "Take your son, your only son Isaac, whom you love, and go to the land of Moriah..."? It is powerfully unnerving to read the laconic conversation between father and son as they ascend the mountain. Children are a most precious gift; Jewish parents are supposed to sacrifice for their children; parents uproot their lives, work long hours, deny themselves luxuries, devote their hearts and minds to enhancing the opportunities that will enable their children to grow up well and prosper.

Profound and universal as such personal feelings are, Abraham's tragedy was more complex.

Isaac represented far more to Abraham than familial and biological continuity and parental love. He was the justification of Abraham's life in more ways than that one's offspring is a source of personal satisfaction and parental fulfillment. Isaac was a tangible emblem of the transcendent purpose held out to his father that he (Abraham) would be a pivotal figure in history in and through the chain of continuity represented by Isaac and Jacob-Israel and the Children of Israel. Human history would be completely different and immeasurably better because of the religion of the descendants that would spring from Abraham's progeny. Certainly Abraham was fully aware of this promised destiny when he climbed the mountain, contemplating having to sacrifice Isaac after he reached the top.

Ten chapters earlier in Genesis, God uprooted Abraham from his home in Haran and sent him wandering in the land of Canaan, promising only that, in that land, his latter-day offspring would be a decisive force in the moral education of humankind. In each story about him, Abraham is depicted as a man of spiritual nobility and the most intense faithfulness. We may infer that the mature Abraham could not have been moved by promises of beautiful concubines, greater physical strength, infinite wealth and political power, or even superhuman intellect. But he was moved by the promise that he would be an ancestor, as Genesis 18:16-17 puts it, of "a great and mighty nation, that all the nations of the earth shall bless themselves by him," and that God chose him "that he may charge his children and his household after him to keep the way of the Lord by doing righteousness and justice." Such a place in history was the ultimate reward to someone who could not be bought by any tangible bribe. In the biblical philosophy of history, time was, in effect, to have been divided into two great periods: before and after God's covenant with Abraham.

The testing of Abraham on Mount Moriah, then, is even more severe than the testing of God's servant Job. The author of the book of Job poses the question, through the mouth of the accusing angel in the heavenly court, whether the rich, happy, healthy, and righteous Job would still be so righteous if his wealth, family, friends, and children were taken away from him. The question posed at the beginning of Genesis 22 is whether Abraham will continue to be quite so true to God's word were he faced with the likelihood that his promised place in history would be denied him. Would Abraham be faithful if his faith that something profoundly new should arise from him would turn out to be empty and vain? Would Abraham continue to be God's servant when confronted, not only with the loss of posthumous fame, but with the abyss of personal meaninglessness entailed by his dying without a worthy heir?

The stories of Job and Abraham, then, pose a perennial question about human nature that resurfaces again and again in literature and life. What can move us to behave disinterestedly, without regard for self, without looking for reward? As the talmudic rabbis express it, what can motivate us to study, worship, act *leshma*, for the sake of God's Name, so that the divine goal of justice and holiness be achieved in the world? Perhaps here is the guts of being religious: why be honest if there is no profit in it and no one will know that we cheated; why be considerate if the reward is in not doing so; why be truthful if we can get away with being false? What do we really stand for in our heart of hearts? According to the Bible, what did Job really stand for? He complained incessantly (fortunately he had a ghost writer with a fine sense of poetry) but he remained faithful to God. According to the Bible, what did Abraham really stand for? Abraham didn't complain to God the way Job did (a midrash suggests that for this reason he was considered more noble than Job). But in his silent acceptance he remained true to the one God he revered -- even faced with the prospect that the sacrifice of Isaac would render his life futile.

The stories of Job and Abraham both have happy endings of sorts. Job is restored. Abraham is told to sacrifice a ram that God has arranged to be there on the spot. At the end of Genesis 22 the promise to Abraham is reaffirmed: "I will indeed bless you, and I will multiply your descendants like the stars of heaven and as the sand which is on the seashore, . . . and by your descendants shall all the nations of the earth bless themselves, because you have obeyed my voice." But the ending is not the point, the experiment is. Being faithful points to a ground of value that remains even with the loss of other meanings, base or noble as they may be. This ground of being is the origin of true religiosity. The endings of the stories of Job and Abraham have their point, however: we are not expected to live solely on that supreme level of ultimate motivation. We have to live in the mundane world, grounded in a higher realm while coping with normal human nature.

We know only too well how self-centered and egotistical people can be, not excepting ourselves. Job and Abraham remind us that we have the capacity not always to be self-regarding, not always to ask "what's in it for me." We offer rewards to train our children (and ourselves) eventually to act without needing to be rewarded. To be sure it is not common to reach this level, but "all things excellent are as difficult as they are rare." Let us listen and thereby gain hope.

(September 25, 1995)

2. The Perspective of the Angel

Over the past more than three decades I have considered the Rosh ha-Shanah Torah reading, the biblical story of the binding of Isaac in Genesis 22, from a number of perspectives: Abraham's, Isaac's, Sarah's, that of the ram that was caught in a thicket at the top of Mount Moriah. But in reading over the story in preparation for this Rosh Ha-Shanah, to my surprise and shock I discovered that we have omitted the crucial perspective of a personage present in verses 11 and 15 of the text: the angel who orders Abraham to desist.

We remember that Abraham is told by God to take Isaac, whom he loves, to the land of Moriah and present him there as an offering. The text tells us that Abraham prepares for the trip, journeys for days with his son, leaves his servants at the foot of the mountain, climbs the trail with Isaac in hand, builds an altar on its height, binds his son on the altar, picks up the knife -- and then, in the eleventh verse, the angel calls to him, "Abraham, Abraham ... Do not raise your hand against the boy or do anything to him, for now I know that you fear God." At that point Abraham notices a ram caught by its horns in the thicket and offers the ram as a substitute. Then the angel calls to him a second time, "By myself I swear, declares the Lord, Because you have done this and not withheld your son, your favored one, I will bestow My blessing upon you and your descendants... and all the nations of the earth shall bless themselves by your descendants..."

Why, at the beginning of the chapter, does the narrator tells us that Abraham receives the initial order directly from God, whereas the dialogue with God at the end is via an intermediary? From the mouth of the angel, and only from his (or her) mouth, comes a statement that Abraham might actually have been willing to complete the sacrifice: "Because you have done this and not withheld your son, I will bestow my blessing upon you and your descendants." Much hinges on how we interpret the seemingly incidental information that these words come from an angel rather than as a direct divine communication. Because it is a hallowed Jewish tradition that no detail in the text of the Torah is to be ignored, this contrast hints at a deeper significance. Before I try to unpack this, I would like to say something about angels.

Many of you have probably gotten your idea of angels from Renaissance paintings -- beautiful little kids, smiling and chubby, winged with halos; or, alternatively, mature, etherial beings ensconced on the clouds, harps in hand or viols da gamba clutched in the folds of their exquisitely painted robes. But the biblical *malakh* is simply a word meaning messenger. Pre-exilic angels (those employed by the deity before 586 BCE) were anonymous but ordinary in appearance, mistaken as human beings until they revealed their special status. *Angelos* is the Greek translation for the Hebrew *malakh*, messenger. Post-exilic angels, in the apocalyptic and classic rabbinic writings, are awesome creatures, personalized as Michael, Gabriel, Raziel, and so forth, employed to guard the heavenly palaces, protect the supernal throne, instruct visionaries, and carry out divine orders. Medieval philosopher-scientists such as Maimonides assured us that *malakhim* were heavenly intelligences, composed of a supraterrestrial matter called the fifth element (the quint-essence) and that, through the love of the Prime Mover, the First Cause, they provide the motive power for the revolving of the heavenly spheres, making them, in Marxist terms, some of the earliest of revolutionary forces. Fashions in angels, like fashions in hair, neckwear, and so much else, change from age to age.

These days, when many find it easier to believe in angels than in God, it is possible to conceive of an angel as an extraterrestrial structure made up of photons, neutrons, positrons, or some yet undiscovered and exceptionally charmed molecular particles, perhaps a form of RAM resident in a point of space smaller than the head of a pin. Entities from another planet, star, or galaxy, these angelic superbrains have assumed an apparent personhood, complete with enlarged cranial cavity and rather anorexic body (at least according to the pictures I have seen), a form of virtual reality that can communicate with much cruder physical beings produced by more normal evolutionary processes of the natural universe. (To be sure, angels would themselves be a product of cosmic evolution, but analogous to a machine-intelligence, cool, dispassionate, 100% rational according to the rules incorporated into their central processing chip, able to perform gigabytic file-saves far beyond ours; with the capacity to organize, in the blink of their supersensitive diodes, global searches throughout the Book of Life; performing merges-sorts, data processing, and spreadsheet calculations that can translate a mathematically optimal solution almost instantly into definitive action as fast as the speed of light.

Such beings must exist because in recent years many people testify to having been abducted by such angelic supra-intelligent creatures who perform mysterious experiments on them in order to figure out what makes such a bizarre creature as a contemporary American citizen tick.

Back to the Akedah.

In my opinion (not to mention that of many of our sages of blessed memory), in light of the subsequent teachings of Judaism about the obscenity of child sacrifice and the sinfulness of killing except in self-defense, we can conclude that God tested Abraham but never intended that he actually sacrifice his son on Mount Moriah. (Why put Abraham, not to speak of Isaac, through the ordeal in the first place? Because in the book of Genesis, God teaches the most important lessons through the unfolding of a story and only later segues into lists of commandments and, subsequently, prophetic oracles and rabbinic discussions, and the homilies of preachers.)

We can also conclude that Abraham knew that, at the end, he would not have to sacrifice Isaac, which would have undone the whole purpose of his life by destroying the people of which he was to be the ancestor. Elsewhere in Genesis we learn that Abraham was quite capable of protesting injustice with all his heart, especially the murder of innocent people in Sodom and Gomorrah. Actually the pace of the text suggests that Abraham was being quite clever in response to God's order: he was using the hallowed bureaucratic strategy of dealing with an apparent irrational or immoral order by a superior: stalling. Rather than challenge the directive head-on, a skillful administrator procrastinates until the boss realizes that the proposal is a bad one, giving the superior a chance to reconsider, save face, and do the right thing. This strategy also makes the bureaucracy maintain a stance of being obedient and respectful, while avoiding direct challenge until things are on the right track again. So Abraham moved slowly, slowly, until the crisis was resolved. The angel, looking on, didn't understand what was taking place between the lines, in the pauses of the text.

Now don't get me wrong. Angels, like computers, can be extraordinarily sophisticated. But at the same time they remain stupid. They have no *sekhel*, no moral imagination, no capacity for regret, outrage, or protest. Angelic computers wait patiently and follow orders.

There are three more points I would like to make about angels.

First, God knows the human heart, but the angels don't (I suppose that is why in recent years they have been conducting those experiments on weird Americans). Thus in Genesis 18:19 God has to explain to the heavenly host Abraham's intent when he insists that the few righteous souls in Gomorrah should be saved before the city is totaled.

Second, angels, who want God's orders to be strictly obeyed, have no ability to temper justice with compassion. Angels don't have an evil inclination because they can't empathize with a person's moral dilemmas. Indeed, in Jewish legend, the angels recommended against the creation of human beings because human beings are so messy, morally as well as physically. Humans sin, but angels can't.

Human beings are conflicted creatures, subject to the pushes and pulls of drives, needs, and desires, summarized in the Jewish tradition as the *yetzer tov* (the good impulse) and the *yetzer ha-ra* (the bad impulse). Human beings have all these ids, libidos, and voracious egos; in their irrationality humans are quite inferior to angels. But human beings are supposed to resolve the tensions between the demands of the body and the spirit, the overlapping of moral claims, the conflict between duty and conscience. In this regard they are superior to the angels in the burden put on them and their occasional ability to rise to its challenge.

Once again, back to the Akedah.

The crux is that the speech of the angel at the end of the story is not, literally, the speech of God. It is what the angel thought that God meant for the angel to say. It is informed by a heavenly perspective but contaminated by a dumb angelic nature. For the angelic mind, the test of the Akedah was one a well-functioning computer passes every day: doing what the creator intended and exactly following keyboard instructions, that is, giving mechanical, unquestioning obedience. From the angel's perspective, Abraham passed because he did what he was told (the angel didn't notice the subtler aspects of Abraham's strategy of procrastination). The angel was tone-deaf to the actual trial that God was carrying out: to examine the depths of Abraham's trust, knowing that, at the same time, Abraham would not commit an immoral act. God knew the full answer because God saw what was in Abraham's mind and heart, not just his behavior: indeed, God might be defined as that supreme entity that can read our minds, including Abraham's mind as he made his way up that mountain.

What about the angel's statement in verse 16, "Because you have not withheld your son, I will bestow my blessing upon you, etc."? The angel interpolated "Because you have not withheld your son" as a result of a limited notion of what God and what Abraham intended. As we noted earlier, angels are smart but dumb -- what can you expect of an oxymoronic machine-intelligence? Elsewhere (in Genesis 26.5) the same "because (*ekev*)" formula is used when it is explained to Isaac that Abraham had kept God's charge, commandments, and laws -- laws which every Jewish commentator agrees included prohibitions on child sacrifice and murder, commandments which would have been plainly violated if Abraham slaughtered Isaac. Abraham did not intend to sacrifice Isaac; God did not intend that he do so; but this is what an angel, capable of only seeing surfaces, might assume.

The angels applauded Abraham for having the very opposite intention from that for which God was rewarding him. Abraham was not a yes-man nor a robot. Abraham was willing to endure the painful dilemma of responding somehow to God's command, trusting that God would never allow killing to occur at the end. I suppose that Abraham knew he was a character in a book, not an algorithm or a set of parameters or a computer protocol. Human life is living in uncertainty, even agony, on the ridge of doubt and faith, remembering what is right and good, trying to do the best we can, with *sekhel*, street smarts, and our moral imagination. Angels we will never be, nor should we. Robots, angels, and computers have their value, but they will never replace us in the higher-order moral cosmos we are forced to inhabit, whether we like it or not.

(September 13, 1996)

3. The Akedah in Christianity and Islam

Genesis 22, the Torah portion for this morning, is a crucial episode in the scriptural portrait of Abraham, the first of several accounts of him in the history of world religions. Besides the biblical depiction there are the later Jewish renditions and the Christian and Muslim versions (I will call them Abraham I, II, III, and IV). All the biblical faiths look back to this figure as, in some sense, the originator of their traditions. They have all been called "religions of Abraham," in contrast to the great religions of the East, such as Buddhism, Hinduism, Confucianism, and Taoism, which conceive of the order of Being out of quite different roots.

Abraham I, the biblical figure:

Avram, our hero's original name, first appears in Genesis 12, when God sends him on his wanderings from Haran to the land of Canaan. In chapter 15, God reiterates to the childless Avram his earlier promise that Avram's offspring will be as numerous as the stars of the heaven. Verse 6 comments: "Because [Avram] put his trust in the Lord, [God] reckoned it to his merit," a verse pregnant with later meanings soon to be explained.

In the next chapter, Avram's wife Sarai turns over to her maidservant Hagar so that Avram might have a son. When a child was born of that cohabitation, Sarai dealt harshly with Hagar. Hagar ran away, only to encounter a messenger of God who promised that her son Ishmael would be the ancestor of the nomads living in the wilderness.

In verse 5 of chapter 17, our hero Avram appears before the Judge of the earth for a name change. God tells him, "You shall no longer be called Abram but Abraham, for I make you a father of a multitude of nations (*av hamon goyim*, a Hebrew play on words without an equivalent in English). I will maintain My covenant between Me and you and your offspring-to-come, as an everlasting covenant throughout the ages . . ." As a sign of that covenant Abraham is commanded to circumcise his male progeny on the eighth day after their birth.

Not long after, Sarai, renamed Sarah, bears to Abraham Isaac, the very lad who is almost sacrificed on Mount Moriah in Genesis 22. As you know -- or will soon happily find out -- at the last moment a ram is substituted, the covenant is reaffirmed, and Abraham and his son return to their encampment. Almost immediately Sarah dies and Isaac acquires a wife, Rebecca. When Abraham dies (chapter 25), the divine blessing passes to his son Isaac and from Isaac to Jacob, renamed Israel, and then to the *Benei Yisrael*, the Children of Israel, and finally to the entirety of *am Yisrael*, the People of Israel.

INTERPRETING THE AKEDAH YEAR BY YEAR

Abraham II, the Christian figure:

Abraham is mentioned 72 times in the New Testament. One of the most important is in the epistle of Paul to the early Christian community in Rome where Paul avers that all Christians, whether or not formerly Jews, are now Abraham's children. The special righteousness ascribed to Abraham in Genesis 15:6 (the verse pointed out earlier) is imparted to all who believe in Jesus as the Christ, the anointed messiah. Romans 4:13-25 states:

> The promise to Abraham and his descendants, that they should inherit the world, did not come through the Law. It came through the righteousness of faith. [Salvation] depends on faith . . . -- not only to the adherents of the law [the Jews] but also to those who share the faith of Abraham, for he is the father of us all, as it is written, "I have made you the father of many nations" -- in the presence of the God in whom [Abraham] believed, [the God] who gives life to the dead and [the God who] calls into existence the things that do not exist. In hope Abraham believed against hope, that he should become the father of many nations; as he had been told, "So shall your descendants be." . . . That is why his faith was "reckoned to [Abraham] as righteousness." The words "It was reckoned to him" were written not for Abraham's sake alone, but for our sake [that is, the Christians] also. It will be reckoned to us who believe in [the God] that raised from the dead Jesus our Lord, [the Jesus] who was put to death for our trespasses and raised for our justification.

In some later Christian writers, Abraham's almost sacrifice of his son Isaac is a foreshadowing of the sacrifice by God of his son Jesus the Christ which atones for sinful humankind. Abraham is a supreme model of faith in God's grace and the religious ancestor of the spiritual Israel, the Christian Church.

Abraham III, the Muslim version:

Abraham is mentioned at least 50 places in the Koran. In Muhammad's version, Abraham built the Kaba, the holy shrine of the caravan city of Mecca, together with his son Ishmael, father of the Arabs. Abraham and Ishmael founded the religion of Islam, *islam* meaning "complete dedication or submission to God." From the sura entitled "The Cow":

> When the Lord put Abraham to the proof by enjoining on him certain commandments and Abraham fulfilled them, God said: "I have appointed you a leader of mankind." . . . We enjoined Abraham and Ishmael to cleanse Our House for those who walk round it, who meditate in it, and who kneel and prostrate themselves. . . . Abraham and Ishmael built the House and dedicated it, saying: "Accept this from us, Lord. You are the One that hears all and knows all. Lord, make us submissive [*muslimim*] to You; make of our descendants a nation that will submit [make *islam*] to You. . . ." Who but a foolish man would renounce the faith of Abraham? We chose him in This World; in the World-to-Come he shall abide among the righteous. When His Lord said to him: "Submit," Abraham answered: "I have submitted to the Lord of the universe."

For Muhammad, the religion of Abraham, the "best religion," is prior to Judaism and Christianity. The purest version of the heavenly book containing God's word is the Koran, the purest religion being based on the laws that it contains or that are derived from it and Muhammad's precedents. The Jewish and Christian scriptures contain some truth but not the most precise and final truth. Abraham stood out as the first of many prophets sent to many peoples in a chain of messengers, the climax and seal of which was Muhammad himself.

In the Koran it is told that Ibrahim received in a dream the order to make a sacrifice to God. He first offered a bullock and then a camel, but God demanded the sacrifice of his son.

His son encouraged Abraham to obey by saying, "Father, take my shirt from my body, lest my dear mother find blood upon it and weep for me. Bind me firmly, so that I do not move, and look away while sacrificing me. Never look at boys of my age, lest grief overwhelm thee!" Three times did Abraham's knife slip while he tried to do the deed, until a voice called, "Ibrahim, Thou hast fulfilled the vision." A ram from paradise was sent down to be offered up instead of the son (*Shorter Encyclopedia of Islam*, 175).

Because one of the key Koran verses does not state explicitly which son was to have been sacrificed, many Muslim theologians explain that the intended sacrifice was actually Isma'il, not Ishak. In any case, the muslimized Abraham is the physical as well as the spiritual progenitor of the Muslim community and a supreme exemplar of compliance to God's will as that faith envisions it.

Finally, the mature Jewish version, *Avraham avinu*, Abraham IV:

Was this Abraham (a) a model of faith, as in the traditional Christian interpretation? Was he (b) a model of obedience in action, as in the Koran? Was he (c) the physical or the spiritual ancestor of the holy people? Was he (d) the first in the direct line of patriarchs and prophets down to Moses, Isaiah, and others who received divine commandments? The correct answer to this multiple choice question is (e) all of the above -- and more.

In Judaism, Abraham is the father of Jews by birth, Jews born of a Jewish parent, and of Jews by choice, proselytes. (To this day converts are given the Hebrew names son or daughter of Abraham and Sarah.) To fulfill the commandment of circumcision is to fulfill a covenantal commitment that God made with Abraham and his descendants. In the traditional high holy day liturgy, Abraham's obedience to God is a source of such vast *zehut*, such vast merit, that it helps atone for the vanities and lies uttered by the people of Israel in this world (*Pesikta de Rav Kahana*, 154a).

The best-known midrash about the young Abraham is in Genesis Rabba, a collection of rabbinic homilies probably compiled in the fourth century CE. (A version of this midrash is found in the Koran, compiled about three centuries later, so that the Muslim conception of Abraham's pure monotheism may have been borrowed from rabbinic Judaism.) In this prequel (to use the movie term), we learn that in Haran Abraham's father was a maker of idols.

> [One day] a woman came carrying a bowl of fine flour and said, "Here, offer it to the gods [of your father]." At that, Abraham seized a stick, smashed all the images, and placed the stick in the hand of the biggest of them. When his father came, he asked: "Who did this to the gods?" Abraham answered.... "[Each of the gods wanted to eat of the flour first until] the biggest of them rose up and smashed all the others." His father replied: "Are you making sport of me? They cannot do anything!" Abraham answered:... "Let your ears hear what your mouth is saying!" (Bialik and Ravnitsky, *Sefer ha-Aggadah*, p.32).

The rabbinic Abraham was not only faithful, obedient, and good -- he was smart, as well.

The greatest of the compliments the Jewish tradition pays to *Avraham avinu* is to conceive of him as the originator of monotheism, the spiritual ancestor of those who believe in one God, who, as the prophets tell us, is a God of righteousness and lovingkindness.

In conclusion: The story that we read now in Genesis 22 implies that the biblical Abraham at first thought that God might actually have wanted him to offer up Isaac as part of a cruel religious ritual widely practiced in the ancient world. The unfolding of the story is a clarification, spelled out in specific injunctions of the Torah, that God certainly does not want child sacrifice: The prophet Micah calls on human beings to pursue justice, love mercy, and walk humbly with God. Abraham's biblical monotheism -- *ethical* monotheism -- is a giant step in a process of theological and intellectual clarification of the new moral world that monotheism helped bring into being, a clarification that will continue as long as the vision of an ideal human life continues to unfold out of this now sacred Abrahamic beginning.

[I would like to acknowledge my indebtedness to Lippman Bodoff's article, "The Real Test of the Akedah" in *Judaism* vol. 42, no. 1 (Winter 1993), 71-92.]

(September 20, 1998)

4. An Indian Akedah

Reading the University of Chicago Press sale catalogue a few months ago, I came across a book with the title *The Hungry God: Hindu Tales of Filicide and Devotion*. (Filicide is in the dictionary, from Latin *filius*, son (as in filial), and *-cide*, killing, as in homicide.) Aha, I thought, material for a new approach to Genesis 22, the binding of Isaac, seeing it from the perspective of similar tales in the Indian religious tradition.

When I received the book I saw my thought was not quite as original as I had hoped. The author, David Shulman, is a professor in the Department of Indian, Iranian, and Armenian Studies at the Hebrew University of Jerusalem. In the preface he remarks, "The following chapters show what happens when one teaches Sanskrit in Jerusalem" where the Akedah story often elicits a rich response.

What benefit is there in looking at the Akedah from the perspective of tales of a South Asian religious tradition that had no direct contact with biblical Israel? In world folklore certain universal themes reappear in many garbs: the flood, the trickster who gets tricked, family rivalries that lead to war or murder, etc.

It is instructive to see how these themes were developed in these different cultures in relation to the values and concerns of each. By examining the Indian tradition on the theme of the filicide as a result of devotion to God, sacrifice to the deity of that which one loves the most, we can see some distinctive features of the way the biblical authors developed the trope.

According to Shulman, there are several versions of the tale of a father who was willing to sacrifice his son for the sake of his religion in the Indian tradition, beginning with the Vedic literature (the Brahmanas) and the epic writings (the Mahabharata), and continuing into the Middle Ages. The version closest to the Akedah is that of a 12th-century Tamil poet Cekkilar in a long work entitled *Periya Puranam*.

Lest I upset you unnecessarily, let me reveal that, horrifying as it is, the tale concludes happily: as with the Akedah, the child is alive and reunited with his family at the end. I intend to omit the more grisly details, even though the tale is probably no worse than can be seen on television or in the movies these days.

Shiva, one manifestation of the Hindu concept of divinity, decides to investigate how far his worshipers will go to worship him. Parancoti, a warrior of a great clan in the Chola kingdom of southern India, is a passionate lover of Shiva. Parancoti is known as the "Little Devotee" for his concern for providing meals to the ardent followers of Shiva. To provide these followers, who wander around as beggar/ascetics and fast for long periods of time, with an occasional meal is a great honor. "In order to savor the love that has the essence of truth," Shiva appears on earth in the form of such an extreme ascetic. He shows up at the Little Devotee's home and indicates that he is willing to be fed by him. The Little Devotee is deliriously happy to be able serve a holy man by feeding him.

Shiva, of course disguised as the ascetic, tells him: "The beast I eat is human, five years old without a blemish, a good child, the only son of a good family. The father and the mother must prepare him." Without hesitation, the Little Devotee rushes home to do the deed. He feels "like someone who has attained a perfect gift," offering to a saint that which he loves best. Father and mother (even the son) all laugh in happiness. "Together, they exulted at heart, performing that difficult deed."

The parents usher the ascetic to table with great deference and ask for permission to serve him the curry they have prepared. "But you must eat with me," the god commands. When the father reaches out to partake, Shiva stops him: "I, an ascetic, eat once in six months, whereas you never miss a meal. Why are you rushing? Call your flawless son to join us." The Little Devotee expresses puzzlement over why, considering the contents of the menu, the ascetic wants the son formally invited. Against all reason, the father and the mother go outside and call, "Come, my son." Out of nowhere, "by the graciousness of God, appears the son beautiful beyond compare."

The Little Devotee rushes back with his son to eat with the holy guest but Shiva and the meal have disappeared. Moments later, Shiva in his divine form appears in the heavens along with his consort and son. Much pleased at their obedience, the God looks with compassion at the Little Devotee and his family "who have melted, in their bones and hearts"; they will never be separated from Him again.

How do the Hindu and the biblical tales compare?

The comparison is not just a matter of a polytheistic versus a monotheistic story. On its most sophisticated level, Hinduism was monotheist. For Shiva's worshipers while they were worshiping him, Shiva was God. But biblical religion was based on an intellectual revolution far more drastic than any other ancient religion experienced: through the concept of "idolatry," they denied the metaphysical reality of all other deities and postulated the divinity of only one God. Shiva's followers never denied that Vishnu was a manifestation of God. Elijah did not admit that Baal was divine.

In Indian tradition Shiva is God of creativity, preservation, and destruction -- especially destruction. Shiva is God as incarnate in the repeated cycle of nature: creation -preservation-destruction-creation-preservation-destruction, personifying the inexorable passage of time and the creation out of destruction of new life. The great dance of reality is symbolized by the iconic form of Shiva Naturaja, Shiva the Lord of the [cosmic] dance. Most of you have seen these depictions of Shiva Naturaja that originated in South India: treading upon a dwarfish figure who is the personification of ignorance, Shiva dances in a circle of fire, clutching in his four arms such symbols as a drum, a club, a skull, or a ball of fire or making hand motions appropriate to the dance of Being.

The biblical God is sovereign and judge of human history par excellence, invisible, immaterial, transcendent of the forces and patterns of nature, manifested primarily through the word -- the word of prophets and of the instructions and commandments of Torah. The biblical God is the creator of the world but the creator of creators who are the actors of history. It is independent meaningfulness of history that is the core of the biblical message, involving the transformation of human nature rather than its submersion into the cosmic pattern. Abraham is to become the ancestor of a people that will bring the moral vision of the one God to all the world -- but this cannot take place if Isaac dies before he has progeny. Were this to happen, the core of history as understood by the biblical authors would be destroyed.

Both religions aver the love of God. The Tamil story described above is part of what is called the *bhakti* tradition in Hinduism, in contrast to the yoga tradition that is best known outside India. The latter is ascetic, concerned with dominating and repressing the senses to achieve, through the mastery of the physical and through meditation, a state of inner tranquility that leads to full consciousness of the Absolute, Brahman. In contrast, the *bhakti* tradition emphasizes emotion, song, prayer, especially communal prayer -- utter devotion to God by people on every level of spiritual achievement. In our tale, the hero and his family are so devoted to Shiva that at the end they are absorbed into Him -- they become part of God which is being-in-itself.

In the Bible we are told to "love the Lord your God with all your heart, all your soul, all your being," but we remain separate creatures from each other and from the divine. Unlike the Little Devotee, who is nothing but joyful in his obedience to Shiva's brutal requests, Abraham seems to be anxious to an extreme as he ascends to the sacrificial location. If we read between the lines, we can sense the tension in Abraham's and Isaac's ascent of the mountain in face of God's irrational instruction. The mood of the biblical tale is far, far darker than that of the Tamil version. The divine instruction seems especially irrational because if Abraham sacrifices Isaac to the God of history, the transcending meaning of his life is destroyed. From Abraham is to come a great people who are to be a blessing to all the nations of the world. This cannot transpire if Isaac is sacrificed. There will be no one to inherit the blessing, to carry on the covenant. Abraham's faith therefore is quite different than that of the Little Devotee. It is faith as hopeful trust rather than as maniac devotion. In my interpretation, it is trust that Abraham *won't* have to sacrifice Isaac, even though how this will occur he doesn't know. (Note that Abraham tells the young men who have accompanied him to the bottom of the mountain that "We will ascend and we will return.")

It is not tragic that Isaac must die. According to the Bible, everyone dies. It would be tragic if Isaac dies before he and his future wife give birth to Jacob, who will continue the chain of ancestors of the future people.

The price Abraham paid for this encounter with the divine will is indicated in Genesis by his death in the very next chapter. Indeed, medieval Jewish midrash say that Isaac, who is described as blind by the time he is blessing Jacob and Esau, became blind as a result of the ordeal on Mount Moriah.

In conclusion: In the Hindu tale, no substitute is provided for the child or legitimized for worshipers thereafter. It is as though Shiva feeds on the love of his followers in a physical sense and then absorbs them spiritually. In the biblical tale, God provides a ram as a substitute for Isaac at the last possible moment when Abraham has bound Isaac on the altar they have constructed on the top of the mountain and has raised his knife over the body of his son. There are references to child sacrifice later in the Bible, but these are appalling and not happy instances. Something like child sacrifice is prohibited in biblical worship. The Akedah is a one-shot event, a unique instance in the historical unfolding the biblical authors cumulatively describe, from Abraham to Moses to the kings of Israel to the Babylonian exile to the restoration to Zion and to the End of Days.

It is particularly significant that we read this biblical story on Rosh ha-Shanah because we will soon listen to the sound of the shofar, the ram's horn, reminding us of the liturgical themes of the 10 days of repentance. In medieval Jewish poetry, God is asked to remember the merit of Abraham and Isaac for their obedience to this strange command and, drawing on their merit, to forgive the sins of their descendants, that is, of us.

(September 12, 1999)

5. The Missing Son

Several months ago I read a review in the *New Republic* of a newly translated book by Yehudah Amichai, *Open Closed Open*, containing several poems on the Akedah. I immediately ordered a copy in anticipation of the New Year Day, 5761. And

I fell in love with his poetry.[3]

One of the greatest Hebrew poets of recent times -- a period which has produced some of the finest Hebrew poetry since the Golden Age of medieval Spain, perhaps since the Bible -- Yehuda Amichai died exactly one week before Rosh ha-Shanah 5761, Sept. 22, 2000. The *New Republic* reviewer, himself a Pulitzer Prize winner in poetry, began his essay by debunking the notion that poetry had to embody "quasi-philosophical counsel." But in the case of Amichai he reversed himself: "There is in . . . poetry such as Yehudah Amichai's *Open Closed Open*, a certain intensity of attention, an ethical focus so absolute that there is no question that significant knowledge is crucially entailed, and wisdom, as a category or a value, seems inescapably germane, no matter how our aesthetic understanding might make us veer away from it. [4] In its remarkably terse and low-keyed way, Amichai's poetry raises us to a higher state of awareness of ourselves as embodied souls.

The short poem that provides the title for the book reads as follows:

> Open closed open. Before we are born, everything is open
> in the universe without us. For as long as we live, everything is closed
> within us. And when we die, everything is open again,
> Open closed open. That's all we are.

---

[3]*Open Closed Open*, translated by Chana Bloch and Chana Kronfield (New York: Harcourt, Inc., 2000). Among other volumes of his poetry in translation: *Yehuda Amichai: A Life of Poetry, 1948-1994*, translated by Benjamin and Barbara Harshav (New York: Harper Perennial, 1994).

[4]C.K. Williams, "We Cannot Be Fooled, We Can Be Fooled," *New Republic* (July 3, 2000), 29.

Conscious that we are caught between two eternities, dwelling in that flicker of time, that small space of history where we are sent or forced to spend our days, we cannot but mutter in the words of that Frank Sinatra song, "That's life."

Another poem of 31 words in English translation captures the human condition through a different set of metaphors:

> Taxis below
> And angels above
> Are impatient.
> At one and the same time
> They call me
> With a terrible voice.
>
> I'm coming, I am
> Coming,
> I'm coming down,
> I'm coming up!

Born in Germany in 1924, Amichai emigrated to Palestine in 1936 and fought in Israel's 1948 War for Independence. Several of his most touching poems deal with seeing his son and daughter off to serve in the Israeli army. His poetry reflects on love and death, the passage of irretrievable time, the clash and the interdependency of the physical and spiritual dimensions of personal existence. At the same time he ties family memories and intimate experiences to the astonishing history of contemporary Israel, to distant places abroad where Jewry once flourished, and, above all, to the Bible. These individualistic themes are laced with biblical phrases and stories appropriated with wit but also with an acknowledgment of pain.

All this probably sounds abstract, but may prepare the ground for two passages of *Open Closed Open* that appropriate the Torah portion for Rosh ha-Shanah morning. In a section of the book called "Jewish Travel: Change is God and Death is His Prophet" Amichai writes:

INTERPRETING THE AKEDAH YEAR BY YEAR

Every year our father Abraham would take his sons to
 Mount Moriah
the way I take my children to the Negev hills where I
 once had a war.
Abraham hiked around with his sons. "This is where I
 left
the servants behind, that's where I tied the donkey to a
 tree
at the foot of the mountain, and here, right here, Isaac
 my son, you asked:
Behold the fire and the wood, but where is the lamb for
 a burnt offering?
Then, up a little further, you asked for the second
 time."
When they reached the mountaintop, they rested a bit,
 ate and drank,
and he showed them the thicket where the ram was
 caught by its horns.

After Abraham died, Isaac started taking his sons to the
 same place.
"Here I lifted the wood, this is where I got out of
 breath,
here I asked, and my father answered: God will see to
 the lamb
for the offering. Over there, I already knew it was me."
And when Isaac's eyes were dim with age, his children
led him to that same spot on Mount Moriah, and re-
 counted for him
all that had come to pass, all that he might have forgot-
 ten.

An exemplar of a truly modern Jew rooted in the riches of Jewishness, Amichai engages in that creative remembering that blends the old and in the new so as to reintegrate them and maintain Judaism as a living tradition. In rabbinic literature, we bring the reality of God into the world. (A famous rabbinic homily on the verse in Isaiah that "You are my witnesses; I am

God" is "When you are my witnesses, I am, as it were, God.") In the section entitled "Gods Change, Prayers are Here to Stay," using the phrase of the Maimonidean confession of faith, Amichai ironically exclaims:

> I declare with perfect faith
> that prayer preceded God.
> Prayer created God.
> God created human beings,
> human beings created prayers
> that create the God that creates human beings.

God made us human, and we make and remake Judaism by creatively remembering. That's what we do here today -- we reread this mysterious tale not just to remember the Binding of Isaac in isolation but in order to remember the need to remember. We do this by measuring ourselves by what we now realize that God wants of us.

Perhaps the most authentic Jewish art form is midrash: searching the text, imaginatively piling the biblical text with new meanings on top of the old ones, uncovering the hidden significance of details and thus reinventing the living meaning of Scripture. In a grouping of poems in *Open Closed Open* called "The Bible and You, the Bible and You, and Other Midrashim," Amichai takes up the Akedah a second time:

> Three sons had Abraham, not just two.
> Three sons had Abraham: Yishma-El, Yitzhak, and Yivkeh.
> First came Yishma-El, "God will hear,"
> next came Yitzhak, "he will laugh,"
> and the last was Yivkeh, for he was the youngest,
> the son that Father loved best,
> the son who was offered up on Mount Moriah.[5]

---

[5]Could this name be a pun on *vayivkeh*, "he cleaved" [the wood], in verse 3?

Yishma-El was saved by his mother, Hagar,
Yitzhak was saved by the angel,
but Yivkeh no one saved.
When he was just a little boy, his father
would call him tenderly, Yivkeh,
Yivkeleh, my sweet little Yivkie --
but he sacrificed him all the same.
The Torah says the ram, but it was Yivkeh.
Yishma-El never heard from God again,
Yitzhak never laughed again,
Sarah laughed only once, then laughed no more.
Three sons had Abraham,
Yishma, "will hear," Yitzhak, "will laugh," Yivkeh, "will cry."
Yismah-El, Yitzhak-El, Yivkeh-El.
God will hear, God will laugh, God will cry.

What can we take away on a Rosh ha-Shanah morning, as we prepare to hear the Binding of Isaac chanted once again? Here is a midrash on Amichai's midrash on the Akedah:

Ishmael, Abraham, Sarah, and Isaac heard God, or thought they did. They laughed with pleasure as the surprises and paradoxes of their lives unfolded: divine promises, blessing, a covenant. Learning that he was to be sacrificed, Isaac was stunned. Thinking that God wanted him to sacrifice a child that was most dear to him, Abraham wept at his loss and Sarah was bereft. Their obedience, rejoicing, and agony reverberate through history, and the echos come back to us. Abraham, the biblical paragon of justice and faith, not only wept but caused God to weep. Sarah suffered silently. Isaac, the link between the generations, forgot and had to be reminded by his children. Remembering is also a bond between humankind and God. For the biblical heroes, it was difficult to become fully human. For God, it was difficult to be God. God's hearing our prayer, laughter at our happiness, and crying at the mess we all too often make of our lives, individually and collectively, have their impact on us and make us more human.

Only through creative remembering can we unite past, present and future. God, who creates our humanity, intensifies these moments of truthful self-examination. We remember to become better, how to be better. We resolve once again, reunify ourselves, and go on.

(September 30, 2000)

ABRAHAM AND THE IDOLS

Robert B. Barr

Abraham had been in his father's idol shop many times. It was a family business. Terah, Abraham's father, had inherited from his father -- who in turn had inherited from his father before him. The designs for the idols sold there had been passed down from father to son for several generations. Though each added some new idols, the historic ones always seemed most in demand.

As it is in most family businesses, everyone had to help. There was much work to be done, and to ensure a profit the family helped out whenever they could. Displays had to be set up, floors swept, records maintained, bills paid, and purchases delivered. For the most part, Abraham was responsible for delivering the idols. Terah would help Abraham load the idols upon a sturdy wooden cart and Abraham would pull it to the home of those who had purchased it. Once the idol had arrived at their home, the family would eagerly assist Abraham at removing the idol from the cart, carrying it to the special place they had selected, and erecting it with the kind of respect and devotion deserving of an idol. Typically, Abraham would just shake his head and leave without uttering a word.

He could not understand those who purchased an idol, nor the reverence which they demonstrated towards it. Abraham knew how the idols were made -- in fact he had helped. For him, the idols were simply stone -- with eyes that could not see, ears that could not hear, mouths that could not speak, and feet that could not move. But still, people would come to his father's shop, reverently touch the idols and pick one which moved them.

Terah had always avoided leaving Abraham alone in the shop for Terah knew of Abraham's disdain for idols and those who would purchase them. But this time Terah had no choice; pressing business on the other side of town demanded his immediate attention and he had been forced to leave Abraham alone.

A sense of dread came over Terah as he neared the store; he knew something was wrong. His steps quickened as Terah hurried to learn what had happened. As he entered his shop, the shop of his father, and his grandfather, he could not believe his eyes. It had been destroyed, displays overturned, walls with holes in them, counters on their sides, and all the idols broken. Once magnificent idols were now shattered pieces of stone. As Abraham stepped out from the back room Terah asked, "who did this horrible thing? Who hated me and my family so much they that would destroy our shop and thus our livelihood?"

Abraham hesitated before answering, "the largest idol did it - he took a hammer and destroyed the others before I could stop and destroy him."

"What, do you take me for a fool," Terah shouted, "these are nothing but stone creations. You destroyed our shop -- you destroyed our family's future."

"If you know that they are but stone," asked Abraham, "why do you sell them? Why do you allow people to believe that they are more than just sculpted rock?"

"It is not my place to take from people that which they hold dear," answered Terah, "I am here to give them what they ask for even though I myself do not believe that what they want is of value."

"That is a sham," declared Abraham, "that is deceitful and dishonest and I will not be a part of such a charade. I will leave this place and I will not return."

With that said, Abraham left his home, his family, his past and began his journey - vowing never to allow the idols of the past to be his security for the future.

Smashing of the Idols - Part II

Thinking he was alone in his father's shop, Abraham began to smash the idols. The man who stood in the entryway unseen was startled by what he saw. Here was Abraham, who was known to be a wise and respectful son, destroying his father's shop. Quickly the man exited and waited to see what would happen. As chance would have it, Abraham's father, Terah was walking down the street.

Standing outside the store, the man watched as Terah entered and surveyed the destruction. He eavesdropped upon the argument that followed between father and son. The man heard Abraham shout - "if you know that they are but stone, why do you sell these idols -- why do you allow people to believe that they are more than just sculpted rock?"

"It is not my place to take from people that which they hold dear," answered Terah, "I am here to give them what they ask for even though I myself do not believe that what they want is of value."

"That is a sham," declared Abraham, "it is deceitful and dishonest - I will not be a part of such a charade. I will leave this place - I will not return."

As Abraham stormed out of the shop the man confronted him -- challenging Abraham for what he had done. The man asked Abraham, "how can you turn your back on the past? How can you reject that which was so important to your ancestors? By rejecting their idols you are rejecting them!"

"No!" declared Abraham, "Not finding value in that which brought my ancestors comfort is not something for which I must apologize. My ancestors found meaning for themselves and so must each person in every generation. We do not dishonor our ancestors when we acknowledge that we find meaning from new sources. We dishonor our ancestors when we feel that the only way to satisfy them is for us to deny who we are and what we believe. We, like they, are on the same quest - seeking truth, gaining wisdom, finding meaning. We are linked -- generation to generation -- by virtue of the questions we ask, not by the answers we find."

"But Abraham," pleaded the man, "what of the past - is it not our responsibility not to forsake it?"

"We do not forsake the past, because we have our own vision of the future," spoke Abraham.

"Our vision inspires us to action - stirs us to meet the challenges of our day - excites us to raise our voices in song so that we may celebrate who we are and that which we are becoming. The past is not forsaken if we are willing to create a future. For in our hearts, and in our souls, and in our minds we will always carry within us those who journeyed before -- those who brought us this far so that we may go even further. Our responsibility is not simply to preserve what came before us: that is the job of idol merchants. We are to build upon what we were given -- not as an act of defiance -- but out of recognition that every generation builds upon the lessons of the past."

By now a crowd had gathered and were listening to the words that Abraham spoke. Some found his declarations heresy. Others simply did not care. And some heard in his words their own thoughts -- and those that did embraced Abraham's vision as their own and together they forged a new path.

Robert B. Barr was ordained by HUC-JIR in 1981. He is the rabbi of Congregation Beth Adam in Cincinnati, Ohio which practices Judaism from a Humanistic Perspective.

COMING HOME TO GLOBAL JUDAISM
YOM KIPPUR MORNING, 5761

Lance J. Sussman

Several years ago, for a variety of different reasons, I decided to develop a survey course on "Religions of the World." Carrying me back to my days as an undergraduate majoring in Religious Studies, it was an immense intellectual undertaking which took the better part of two summers to complete. I soon found myself confronting a galaxy of very challenging questions:

How do scholars study religion today?
What is the best definition of the word "religion?"
When did religion begin historically?
Are all religions really the same?
Is religion bad science?
Does religion cause war or teach peace?
Is religion real or invented?
What is the role of gender in religion?
Is religion growing or dying today?
Is each religion truly unique?
Is comparative religion possible?
Why do Buddhist monks wear orange robes?
What is religious art?
Is the Bible story, fact or fraud?
How many sacred mountains are there?
Is a mezuzah on the White House door constitutional?

As I gained experience with my class, I increasingly noticed interdependencies among world religious traditions. Hinduism was not only shaped by India but by Indo-European immigration, Hellenism, Islam and the British. The Sikh tradition of India combines karma and monotheism. Judaism has been challenged by Hellenism, Persian religions and science. China's spiritual life looks like a cord with three threads – Dao, Confucian and Buddhist – woven together. Many primal religious traditions are regaining spiritual influence among secular 21st century people.

This year, I have the good fortune of teaching "World Religions" to over 250 students, half of whom are Christians, 10% of whom claim they have no religion, several of whom are Korean Baptists who want to learn about their Buddhist grandparents, Copts, Jains, Orthodox Jews and a Catholic who practices her own brand of Methodism.

One of my three TAs is the Imam of the mosque here in Binghamton; another is a secular Turkish woman who told me she votes for the Moslem party at home and the third TA is a Yiddish-speaking woman from Mexico City.

For sure, the sociology of my class is as complex as the content of the class' curriculum. In other words, it would be fair to say that religion today is a complex, post-modern reality in both the most traditional and the most *avant*—sectors of society.

What have I learned about religion by teaching religion globally?

Religion is old – more than a 100,000 years old.

The oldest evidence for religion is Neanderthal burials.

People, as a species, are religious.

Religion can be defined as the construction of a cosmos of meaning in story, song and space.

Religion is inseparable from community, easy to corrupt, impossible to suspend.

No religion is primitive.
The Hindu mind is infinite.
Jainism taught us the principle of non-violence.
Everyone believes in kindness.
Medieval cathedrals are magnificent.
Daoism understands reality.
Islam and Judaism are religious cousins.
Religious violence is unforgivable.
No one religious tradition can represent all of humanity.
All of humanity is represented in almost every religious tradition.

I have also discovered that teaching and studying the religions of the world is not only an intellectual and pedagogical challenge for me, it is also a Jewish challenge for me. Teaching World Religions raises the question of the universal. It challenges the specificity of the Jewish!

How can my home tradition, representing a mere .2% of humanity, make any claim to religious seniority, superiority or special status?

Is being Jewish really anything more than an act of stubbornness, pride or loyalty?

Is there anything to commend Judaism in the worldwide web of spiritual wisdom?

Why should I click on Torah.org and not Hindunet or Koran.com?

While my annual excursion to the international mall of world religious traditions is unusual in its religious focus, it is not necessarily all that different from the vast variety of life experienced by so many of you in the worlds of business, the professions, education, the arts and even a few diverse residential neighborhoods in the Southern Tier.

Today, the whole world constantly presents itself to us in its totality on a daily basis.

We live in a global village, with 24/7 international news, cyberlinks on everything. We can even shop in ethnicized food stores in Johnson City with abundant sushi, Polish and Caribbean products.

In this huge, diverse, changing mix of food, facts and futures, where can Judaism possibly fit into our lives, our minds, our souls?

I think for the vast majority of us, the search and the confirmation of answers, focuses on the Day of Atonement.

Yom Kippur is more than a day on the calendar.

Yom Kippur is about universal questions, about personal performance, about ethics, about sin.

Yom Kippur is about Jewish responses to human challenges.

The Yom Kippur formula is to stand before God of the universe as the children of Israel and ask how we are doing as human beings.

Remarkably, Judaism as practiced on its most sacred day is all about the experience of the universal in the particular.

Experiencing the "universal in the particular" is very different than seeking to isolate, emphasize and enlarge the role of just the particular. Jewish particularism, in particular, has been the principal goal of much of Jewish life in the last 70 or 80 years, a reaction against the grand Jewish universalism of an earlier generation. Zionism, Bundism, American Jewish ethnization have been the principal sociological goals of the organized Jewish community for generations. One leading architect of American Jewish civil policy, Jonathan Woocher, influenced the Jewish federations of North America about 20 years ago to define them principally in terms of "sacred survival." Particularism, American Jews, have heard for years, is the essence, the goal, and the purpose of organized Jewish life.

The modern streams of Judaism also adopted parallel sociological approaches to Jewish existence. Samuel Cohon, author of the Reform platform of 1937 coined the expression, "Judaism as a Way of Life." Mordecai Kaplan talked about "Judaism as a civilization," that is a vast, global expression of the particular. The leading Reform theologian of our own time, Eugene Borowitz, increasingly speaks about Judaism as a "covenantal community" whose principal task is to define its theological and sociological particularism. In many different places, Borowitz has spoken up against the modern and the rational as overly universalistic and, therefore, inimical to the best interests of Jews and Judaism.

On this Yom Kippur, on this day of days, I must wonder aloud about the relationship of the universal and the particular in the contemporary Jewish experience. I have to wonder aloud if Eugene Borowitz and others are right when they say that liberal Jews can no longer organize themselves around ideas like "ethical monotheism" because the idea of "ethical monotheism" can exist without Jews and that Judaism can and must exist only because of itself. I must wonder aloud if this ideological and ethnic conceit is how I really understand the Jewish experience.

In my opinion, using Yom Kippur as our model, it is time to return to a universal, rational, modern framework for understanding Jewish life. Judaism is valid because it embodies truths and values which are valid for everybody, compelling for anybody and necessary for somebody or at least for the Jewish people. An opposing idea now popular among many of the highest level leaders in the Reform movement asserts that Judaism is a universe unto itself which cannot and should not judged by any standard cultural or scientific construction of reality. This strikes me as not only false but also delusional and dangerous.

Unlike Borowitz and his followers in the Reform movement, I do not believe that all of modernity has failed the Jewish people and Judaism because the Holocaust took place in the 20th century. Auschwitz is not the representative expression of modernity. It might not even be an expression of modernism at all.

But, most of all, the Holocaust should not be used as an excuse to abandon the modern, the universal and the rational. Indeed, perhaps the exact opposite is true. Perhaps, we need to look beyond the subjective, selective and nonrational as the building blocks of Judaism of the next century.

In my opinion, it is more than OK, perhaps even necessary, to rearticulate an essential Judaism in modern, liberal terms. Following the masterful example of Dr. Leo Baeck, the rabbi of Berlin and Thereseinstadt, we can begin by acknowledging the mystery and grandeur of creation. Judaism begins with poetry. Judaism begins with the prayerful response. Judaism begins with silence and Judaism begins with song.

Our response to the miracle of existence, however, is not limited to the mystical and can and must include ethical, rational and scientific levels of analysis and development. In Reform Judaism, we believe that we are endowed by our Creator with the ability to create and to use many conceptual tools. To be human is to be a tool user. Let us give honor to our maker not by resorting to selectivity of purpose and style but by defining our quest as broadly as possible.

Finally, let us restore a vision of the future to our Judaism. Traditional Judaism speaks in terms of a personal Messiah. Zionism sees the Jewish state as the vanguard of Jewish messianism. By contrast, contemporary Diaspora survivalism and neo-traditional Reformism has no vision of the future at all. It either begins or ends with the tribe or is perversely narcissistic.

A philosophy of Judaism committed to the "eternal now" which has no vision of the future, no messianic purpose, no redemptive goal will tarry for the night and disappear. It is not a Judaism worthy of our loyalty. It is time for us to go back to early views of the future as envisioned by our great prophets.

Isaiah was a Zionist but he knew that ultimately the goal of Zion was transcendent. Isaiah was a mystic and priest but he despised spiritual narcissism. Isaiah was a prophet who understood that the frontiers of time were also the pathways to the establishment of truth, justice and peace as goals of human society.

Redemption in essential Judaism is not an after thought, a social action program or a liturgical metaphor late in the day. Redemption is the reason we open the door of the synagogue for business, teach our children to follow in our footsteps and what we offer to those in need or distress.

A rational, essential modern Judaism is not to be confused with a mere moralism or Unitarianism or Ethical Culture. It fully honors the specific, the particular, the national, the ethnic, the *heimish* and even the mystical in Judaism. But it does more than that. It rises to the universal, the cosmic, the galactic. It proclaims that Judaism is a tradition worthy of our enduring support because its metaphysic, its ontological presuppositions, its depth reality is at one with the whole universe.

Either what we call Torah is true by any standard, or it is not Torah. Other people, other traditions find their way to the heart of the universe by following their own path. The path of Dao. The path of Ma'at. The path of Dharma. Each path is valid. Each path is adorned with rich tapestries of spiritual self-expression.

The Jewish path is Torah

Every year I tour pathways blazed by other pilgrims. The view from mountaintops of Tibet is liberating. The waters of the Ganges are eternal. The sound of the Imam at prayer is transcendent. In each one is the spark of the divine. But I can only have one home in this world.

On Yom Kippur, I come home. From this place, I thank God for the spiritual diversity revealed through humanity. From this place, I thank God for the heritage bequeathed to me and freely chosen by others. The heritage that heard the call to justice in the silent voice that echoed on Mt. Sinai, echoes still in this sanctuary.

O people of Israel, you are called to serve your God with deeds of lovingkindness and a contrite spirit everyday of your life. Wherever you stray, your God waits for you there.

And at the end of this day, as we prepare to hear the Shofar for the last time, let us affirm without reservation the great affirmation of the prophet Elijah and final response of these days of awe:

> *"Adonai, hu ha-eloheem"*
> "Adonai," the name we call God in Israel,
> "Adonai" is *eloheem*, the great principle of the
>   universe,
> the Ultimate Reality.

Our God, God of all People, on this Day of Atonement, we pray for all people. Establish justice in the gate and peace in the hearts of all your children.

Turn the hearts of your children to their parents and the hearts of parents to their children. Bring us atonement for our misdeeds and at-one-ment with one another and with you. Amen.

A NEW JEWISH AWAKENING

Samuel N. Gordon

Imagine a time in American Jewish communal life when analysts are predicting the imminent decline and demise of the American Jewish community due to assimilation, intermarriage, and religious indifference. Nearing the end of the century, a generation or two removed from the immigration experience, American Jews are now largely accepted socially, academically, and professionally. Feeling welcome and secure as American Jews, too many have become passive and indifferent about their Jewish identity. There is little Jewish practice in the homes, and formal Jewish education is woefully inadequate and widely criticized. Many think that American Jewish life is on an inevitable decline and will fade away amidst the hospitable atmosphere of America.

I am not speaking of the communal reaction to the CJF National Jewish Population Study of 1990. Rather I refer to the concerns and worries of the American Jewish community in the decades following the American Civil War. The widely accepted view has been that the acculturated German American Jewish community of the 19th Century was rescued from total assimilation by the fortuitous arrival on these shores of new Jewish immigrants from Eastern Europe. The new Americans were the salvation of American Jewish life. According to this view, without the mass immigration of observant, traditional, Yiddish speaking Jews, American Judaism would have died.

Jonathan Sarna has recently refuted that analysis and offers a far better understanding of the great Jewish revival, renewal, and awakening of the late 1890's. More importantly, what he teaches about that time period is instructive and relevant for us. In his essay, *A Great Awakening, The Transformation that Shaped Twentieth Century American Judaism and its Implications for Today,* Sarna notes the significant change in American Jewish life, institutions, and commitments that took place in that time period. The renewal movement was already in progress before the immigrants came, and those who led the movement were largely young, native born, Reform Jews of Philadelphia and New York. They were the very ones who had been thought most likely to have assimilated and lost any connection with Jewish life.

A Jewish renaissance and revival was being shaped as early as the mid 1870's. In many ways this movement in American Jewish life was reflective of similar trends in American Protestant life. The First and Second Great Awakenings of American Protestantism resulted in the establishment of schools of higher learning, new congregational movements, mission societies, camp revival meetings, and a general spirit of religious renewal. Similarly a group of young American Jews began to create the great institutions of American Jewish life that we continue to rely on today. Concerned with a lack of spiritual focus, they sought to redefine Jewish life in religious, cultural, and educational ways.

Beginning in the late 1890's, they established such critically important new organizations as the Jewish Publication Society, The American Jewish Historical Society, Gratz College, the Jewish Chatauqua Society, and the National Council of Jewish Women. Cyrus Adler, one of this movement's key leaders, spoke of an American Jewish renaissance and revival. According to Jonathan Sarna, American Judaism was "experiencing a period of religious and cultural awakening, parallel but by no means identical to what Protestantism experienced during the same period." This Jewish great awakening profoundly transformed American Jewish life and reawakened in its followers a return to a spiritual, national, and religious definition of Judaism.

These young, prosperous, and secure American Jews, led by Mayer Sulzberger, Solomon Solis-Cohen, Cyrus Adler, and others were all involved in the Young Men's Hebrew Association of Philadelphia and from that base led a campaign to revive Chanuka as the great Jewish national holiday in order to "revitalize and deepen the religious and spiritual lives of American Jews."

They created the Jewish Theological Seminary and led the movement to bring Solomon Schechter to America. They established an intellectually significant Jewish newspaper, the *American Hebrew*. Their poet laureate was the young Emma Lazarus. Other women became key leaders of this awakening. The National Council of Jewish Women was created in 1893. Reflecting the urban missionary work of Protestant and Catholic women, the synagogue sisterhoods were born. The foreign missions of Protestant women were paralleled in Hadassah, founded by Henrietta Szold, an early member of the awakening group.

Sarna's article is instructive for us because it speaks of a time similar to our own when many thought that American Judaism was in great danger. They did not necessarily use the term "continuity," but they too were worried about the future of American Judaism. What is most significant in Sarna's analysis is his recognition of the true cyclical nature of Jewish history as opposed to the linear view of history that most Jewish historians seem to posit. The linear view holds that American Jewish life moves in a straight line over several generations from an authentic immigrant-based Orthodoxy to Conservative practice to Reform to secularism to total assimilation. In contrast, historians of American Christianity have written of a cyclical pattern of revival and stagnation. There are times of religious renewal and awakening followed by other times of religious indifference.

We, as observers today, might do well to see a similar cyclical pattern in American Jewish life. While there is great concern over Jewish continuity, we are at the same time witnessing one of the potentially great Jewish revivals and renewals in history. Jewish American history does not in fact move along an inevitably declining path from the spiritually engaged generation of our sainted grandparents to the future generation of alienated, assimilated and ungrateful children. I hope to show that Jewish renewal and revival are taking place even amidst those aspects of change that seem most threatening. I would like to examine the assumptions we have been making about intermarriage as one example of the changing face of the American Jewish community, and then I will speak of the synagogue as an example of how a critical institution in our culture must adapt and change in order to nurture a revitalized Jewish life.

A significant debate is taking place in our community over how to react to the phenomenon of intermarriage. For some, the incidence of intermarriage is evidence of a major decline in American Jewish life. Others, however, perceive this as a challenge and even as an opportunity to enrich and expand Jewish life.

Jack Wertheimer of the Jewish Theological Seminary and Steve Bayme of the American Jewish Committee have articulated a position that is opposed to communal resources and energies being focussed on the intermarried and the "marginal." In their five point Statement on Jewish Continuity, they suggest that Jewish communal resources would be better used in serving the moderately affiliated rather than in trying to attract the marginally Jewish or convert non-Jewish spouses. They have long held that efforts at outreach are counter productive and serve only to encourage and sanction intermarriage. Egon Mayer, Director of the Jewish Outreach Institute, argues a very different position. He believes that outreach to the intermarried will have a positive impact on Jewish choices being made by those families. I happen to side with Egon Mayer, and I strongly disagree with Steve Bayme and Jack Wertheimer.

This is a relevant topic for us today for a number of reasons. If we are trying to deal with a changing Jewish world, the issue of intermarriage is one of the best examples of how American Jewish life is radically different from our culture and society a generation ago. We will be forced to set priorities for funding programs that serve this different Jewish world. Should we be concerned with those who seem to have rejected their Jewish roots, become disengaged and alienated, or should we invest more of our resources in serving the moderately committed members of the core group?

A key mistake is being made at the heart of this debate. It is assumed that intermarriage equates with assimilation. It is stated as a given that intermarriage rates are equal to rates of Jewish abandonment and rejection. Most importantly, it is suggested that there will be a near certain loss of positive Jewish identification among the children and grandchildren of the intermarried.

It may well be true that the grandchildren of intermarried couples who were studied for the 1990 CJF census failed to identify as Jews. But let us look at the data on which this conclusion is based. The grandchildren studied must be, by definition, the products of weddings that took place in the 1930's and 1940's. That was an era very different from our own. Many of those intermarrying at the time may well have been seeking to escape from their Jewish roots. Even more importantly, most intermarriages were met with condemnation and rejection from both the Jewish family and community. Certainly there were no programs of outreach to the non-Jewish partner. There were no attempts to help them lead Jewish lives, create Jewish homes, or raise Jewish children. The American Jewish community of the

1930's and 1940's treated intermarriages exactly as Jack Wertheimer and Steve Bayme suggest we treat them today. The result is that the grandchildren of those unions do not identify as Jews. But we cannot extrapolate from those statistics that grandchildren of today's intermarriages will not be Jews. If we create an atmosphere where non-practicing, marginal Christians married to Jews are welcome and supported in their choice to raise Jewish children, then the results could be vastly different from those of the past.

 Intermarriage need not equate with assimilation. Jews who marry non-Jews are not rejecting or abandoning their Jewish traditions. The non-Jewish partner in the intermarriage is often quite willing to raise Jewish children, establish a Jewish home, and identify with Jewish life. More significantly, the non-Jewish partner often seeks a more intensely spiritual, faith centered Judaism than many Jews by birth.

 Intermarriage and the increasing involvement of inter-married families is a major change in American Jewish life. If Wertheimer and Bayme were right, and the intermarried were marginal to Jewish life, there would be no issue of their seeking roles in synagogues or on communal boards. The truth is, they are actively involved in our synagogues, schools, community centers, and charitable organizations. More importantly, few, if any, of our families do not include members who were not born as Jews. Even now, and certainly more in the future, at least half of those worshiping in the sanctuaries of Reform, Reconstructionist, and Conservative synagogues will not have been born as Jews. That is a key factor in our very different Jewish world. It will demand a changing outlook from us. Can we have a Judaism that is not dependent on cultural memories of grandparents who spoke Yiddish, of parents who recalled personal anti-Semitic injustices, of food memories and family stories? Can a former Catholic from Bridgeview or a Presbyterian from Lake Forest raise authentic Jewish children?

Our community must adapt to diversity. The profile of our Jewish families will be strikingly different from the past. In certain sectors of our community the change will be seen as a great threat to Jewish distinctiveness. Boundaries are being breached, and that is seen as dangerous for the viability of Jewish institutional life. But for others, the entry of new Jews as well as those seeking to support Jewish life has added a vibrancy and vitality to our community. In creating a more meaningful, spiritually enriched Judaism, we are attracting many supporters to our cause and in fact experiencing a new awakening in American Jewish life. Jews-by-Choice as well as many non-Jewish partners in Jewish marriages are often the cause of a deepened appreciation for Judaism among their partners who are Jews by birth.

Not everyone is comfortable with this new diversity. This will not be the same Jewish world, but that is not the same as saying that there will be no Jewish world. The comedian, Aaron Freeman, has said that the only problem being Black, Jewish and living in Highland Park is that at this time of the year he has to explain to his children why they can't have a Christmas tree, while their next door neighbors, the Rosenbergs, do. Thirty years ago, no one could have imagined such a scenario.

We need to recognize that changing world. My Jewish world is the universe of the synagogue. It is the setting in which I work and the one that I think about the most. I want to speak of the synagogue as an example of a key Jewish communal institution that needs to change in radical ways. You can extrapolate from the example of the synagogue to the other institutions of Jewish life. I find the synagogue both frustrating and exciting. It is the most important Jewish institution for nurturing Jewish identity and providing spiritual meaning, but it also is seen as a place of boredom, judgementalism, and irrelevance. I remain committed to the synagogue because I think it can change, and if it does it will have the greatest impact on American Jewish life.

Twenty years ago museums of natural history and science were dark cavernous halls in which a person would silently walk past dinosaur bones and passively stare at immovable exhibits. The Shedd Aquarium was a series of dark rooms with aquariums set in the walls. Today, the Field Museum and the Shedd Aquarium are very different places. The same is true of art museums, children's museums, history centers, and many other settings in which we find personal growth and stimulation.

Museums have come to realize that their constituents are interested in participating in active ways in their education. People expect to be engaged and stimulated. They work together in family groups creating projects or discovering new knowledge. At the Field Museum, one is able to pull a stone from the pyramids or draw water from an ancient well, or make a rubbing from a stone monument.

In synagogues, however, we are still walking people past dinosaurs. Too often congregants are expected to be passive listeners and uninvolved parents. Techniques for active engagement are not tried. The synagogue as an institution is slow to change, but its constituency is rapidly changing. With limited leisure time and family time, Jews have many options for personal fulfillment and spiritual growth. If the synagogue is boring and non-responsive, if it is a place where one is made to feel unwelcome, condemned, and judged as inadequate, then people will not choose to be active participants.

On the other hand, the synagogue has great potential for influencing lives. It is usually the most easily accessible Jewish institution in an area. In most urban and suburban centers, there are many choices that one can make based on denomination, location, peer group, or leadership. It is usually child friendly and is often programmatically diverse. But it is also very slow to change, and change it must.

A NEW JEWISH AWAKENING

The American synagogue as we know it was also designed to mirror the American Protestant church, but from a 19th Century perspective. In the late 1800's the opera house and Chatauqua lecture hall were the popular centers of entertainment and enrichment. People expected to listen quietly and passively to concerts and sermons. It is not the model that excites most of us today.

The supplementary religious school is even more anachronistic. Afternoon Hebrew school was established in order to convince Eastern European Jewish immigrants to send their children to public school. It was intended as an alternative to parochial *yeshivahs* and *heders*. With the Hebrew school, immigrant parents were willing to allow their children to attend American public school while they would continue to receive a Jewish education as well. In other words, the original purpose of synagogue supplementary education was assimilation. The goal was to have the immigrant children learn how to be good Americans in public school. It was a fabulous success.

Our needs today are very different, however. In most synagogue schools children do not arrive familiar with Jewish life and practice from a Jewishly active home. Instead, parents often send their children to the school motivated by a sense of obligation to repeat rituals that they themselves resented or rebelled against. In contrast, Jewish adults are seemingly more interested than ever in Jewish learning. Additionally, parent toddler programs, children's museums, and other family activities have provided models of parents and children spending time together in learning and doing.

Our goal is certainly not to acculturate our children as Americans. We are trying to help provide a positive Jewish identity. The best way to do so is by helping parents be the teachers of Judaism to their children. We can increase the comfort level of the family with Jewish practice and action. We can help them find meaningful family expression through Jewish ritual that is simple and enjoyable. The synagogue can be an agent for empowering and enabling Jewish parents to live Jewishly with their children and be the true transmitters of Jewish values, but we must move from a supplementary religious school system that is inherently flawed to a family education model that is revolutionary and exciting.

But the synagogue must also be more than a religious center designed for the typical Jewish family of two parents raising their own children at home. That "normal" Jewish family is approximately 17% of the population. Once more we are confronted with diversity and change. From intermarriage, conversions, re-marriage, blended families, married with no children, empty nesters, never married, gay and lesbian, and many other alternatives, it is clear that any institution designed for the old "typical" family will fail to serve the majority of our population.

Some synagogues view this situation with fear and concern. The truth is that it provides wonderful opportunities for multiple support, study, and discussion groups. Robert Wuthnow, a religious sociologist in the Protestant world, in his book, *Sharing the Journey, Support Groups and America's New Search for Community*, writes of the importance of small groups such as *havurot* in the quest for spirituality. Four out of every ten Americans belong to a small group that meets regularly whether for Bible study, various twelve-step programs, spiritual growth, education, or service. Many churches have successfully incorporated such groups into their mission. Fewer synagogues have done so.

The potential for change is there. Synagogue 2000 is one example of the communal commitment for creating new models for synagogue life. Through the support of the Nathan Cummings Foundation, the Righteous Persons Foundation, and the Shirley and Arthur Whizin Trust, Synagogue 2000 is attempting to develop an "itinerary of change" in the areas of prayer, study, good deeds, and healing.

In my own experience, the area of funding must also change. A set imposed dues structure is perhaps the most resented aspect of American synagogue life. The marginal and alienated who seek, however tentatively, to enter the synagogue are met with an entry barrier and disincentive to membership. We define synagogue membership based on those who pay dues rather than on those who participate. If the synagogue can be made a place of spiritual engagement, personal growth, and emotional support, members will voluntarily contribute based on a sense of investment and commitment.

We are being offered an opportunity to transform American Jewish culture for the Twenty First Century. Rather than be paralyzed by the frightening aspects of change we cannot control, we can instead become agents for positive change and growth. Continuity must not be perverted into stagnation. This is not the first time when Jewish leadership demanded vision. There are those who claim that Judaism's primary strength has been its loyalty to its past and its immutable rules and regulations. But there is another view that sees in Jewish history a record of dynamic change and transformational growth.

In the year 70, with the destruction of the second Temple and the exile from Jerusalem, Judaism might have died, but Yohanan ben Zakkai and his followers reacted to the crisis with extraordinary foresight. They forged a new Judaism wherein synagogues replaced the Temple, rabbis replaced priests, and prayer was the substitute for sacrifice.

In 1492, the vital intellectual and spiritual center of the Jewish world was lost. The Jewish people were forced into exile from Spain, and they too felt abandoned by God just as had those in the time of the Temple's destruction. But in a little town high in the hills of Galilee a small band of mystics gathered around their rabbi, Isaac Luria, the "Ari", and redefined worship and Shabbat, reflecting their intensely personal and intimate relationship with God.

In the late 1600's, the Jewish world was profoundly embarrassed by the false messiah, Shabbatei Tzvi. Perhaps hundreds of thousands had been seduced by his offers of salvation and a return to Jerusalem. The Jewish world was full of disillusionment and cynicism, but then a new populist mystic, the Baal Shem Tov, created a form of Judaism that spoke to the simple people who sought meaning and joy in their life.

A new but very different crisis confronted the Jews of Western Europe at the end of the Eighteenth Century. Instead of servitude and rejection, Jews were now offered freedom and equal rights. Rather than being forbidden to practice their faith, they were given the option of voluntarily abandoning it. Reform Judaism sought to create a modern faith consistent with the values of both the Enlightenment and the Hebrew prophets.

When European liberalism failed, Theodor Herzl dreamed of a Zionism that would transform the individual Jew as well as Jewish life. In less than fifty years, his dream was realized. Israel has created a very changed Jewish reality for us all.

And today American Jewish life and society are also different. There is much about our Jewish culture that would be unfamiliar to our grandparents, but that does not mean that our Jewish world is less authentic or valid. There is a vitality and spirit of renewal today that is energizing many of us in the Jewish world.

Walk into any major bookstore and go to their sections on Jewish thought. Look at the books. See what is being published, sold, and read. Imagine another time when a new translation of the Torah such as Everett Fox's would have quickly sold out its first printing. Look at the number of books about Genesis or the Steinsaltz Talmud or books by Harold Kushner, David Wolpe, Arthur Waskow, or any number of others, and you will see a Jewishly vibrant world. There are serious text study groups meeting in law offices, in homes, at bookstores, and on the internet. More undergraduates and graduate students are studying Jewish thought than ever before.

Institutional Jewish life is witnessing the birth of some remarkable new organizations that are not mere replacements of the old but are helping redefine Jewish life. New Israel Fund, the Jewish Fund for Justice, and Mazon have succeeded in creating new outlets for *tzedakah* and action. The Shefa Fund is an example of a public Jewish foundation moving the Jewish community forward in investing in community development and growth. The National Center for Jewish Healing has profoundly shaped the way in which rabbis and other Jewish professionals deal with the spiritual needs of their congregants. Private Jewish foundations such as Wexner, Bronfman, and Covenant are supporting creative and dynamic work in Jewish education and learning. And the Jewish Funders Network is an organization that is helping a key element in American Jewish life act as catalysts for change and advocates for renewal.

The ultimate goal of creating and nurturing this new Jewish culture must be to transform people even more than institutions. For those of us engaged in leadership, this work must be a reflection of our own personal quest for meaning and spiritual fulfillment. Out of our own commitment to *tzedakah* we can recognize our partnership with God in *tikkun olam*, the repair of our imperfect world. It is an opportunity for us to be agents for change, helping to transform our Jewish world.

Jonathan Sarna stated that a small group of late nineteenth century American Jews successfully reinvented American Judaism. They created a Jewish Great Awakening. But they did more than transform American Jewish society. In the process they transformed their own lives. Let the examples of Emma Lazarus, Henrietta Szold, Louis Brandeis, and their contemporaries inspire us as well. We too have the opportunity to transform our lives as we help prepare American Judaism for the twenty first century.

Samuel N. Gordon was ordained by HUC-JIR in 1980. He is the rabbi of Congregation Sukkat Shalom in Chicago, Illinois. Rabbi Gordon founded Sukkat Shalom, which specializes in family education and in integrating families with diverse religious histories.

PEACE AND THE RELIGIOUS QUESTION

Uri Regev

As I write this article, the missiles, bullets, stones, Molotov Cocktails and other "creative" methods of expressing rage that have come to define the complex relationship between Israel and the Palestinians continue to exact a heavy toll on the region. This article is inspired by the conviction that peace and co-existence must, and *will* ultimately reign in our region. Even if brotherly love is too great a goal for the near future, both sides *will* return to the negotiating table and find a way to restore their relationship in such a manner that will allow the two peoples to exist side by side with dignity and mutual respect for one another.

Ours is a region and a people all too familiar with crises and setbacks, and I am convinced that this setback too will be surmounted, despite the sorrow which will be indelibly etched in the memory of a generation. It is our fate to share the tiny strip of land, and no one will succeed in removing the other by use of force, even if some would believe otherwise.

Since religion is one of the caustic elements underlying the crisis, immediate attention must be dedicated to it for the sake of our future together. The negative effects of religious fundamentalism holds particularly true to the Palestinian Authority, as it is well known that religious incitement resonates through the mosques, radio, television broadcasts which teach Palestinian youth that as "martyrs" who die while battling Jews, their entry into heaven is assured. The hate and anti-Semitism instilled into pupils poisons the hearts and minds of Palestinian youth and adults, and contributes greatly to their resistance of the peace process and especially to the present violence.

Religious fundamentalism must be eradicated, as the failure to combat this will effectively remove any prospect of peace. It is deplorable that those tolerant voices that interpret Jihad as a spiritual battle, one which sanctifies life and peace, are silenced by extremism. The path of peace implores us to strengthen and insure the expression of these voices.

While we may find ample justification for holding the Palestinian Authority responsible for many of the region's woes, the Jewish religious sector, too, is culpable, in that it has not always played a positive role in the relations between the two nations, and has not prepared its adherents for peace or even emphasized its desirability. I will focus in this brief article on the connection between issues of religion and state and the future of peace and the relations between Jews and Arabs. I will suggest that strengthening Jewish pluralism and the Reform Movement in Israel are not only contributions to strengthening democracy and religious freedom in Israel, but are essential to ensuring peace and a bright future for our region.

With uncertainty currently reigning in Israel, the only constant is the state of perpetual vacillation that has come to define the public mood. The road to peace has been beset with obstacles, and the euphoria of the famous handshake of the Israeli Prime Minister and the Palestinian chairman on the White House lawn has long since faded. The Israeli Prime Minister was since assassinated by a religious fanatic who argued for the religious justifications of his actions, comparing himself to the biblical figure of the zealot priest Pinchas, who assassinated the fornicating Jewish prince Zimri and Cozbi, the daughter of the Medeonite tribe head. Rabin's assassin claimed that as a religious zealot special laws applied to him, a claim unfortunately rooted in our religious tradition.

PEACE AND THE RELIGIOUS QUESTION

The correlation between religious leanings and attitudes towards the peace process becomes clear when observing public pronouncements made by the religious leadership. A number of years ago, the Tami Steinmetz Institute of Research at Tel Aviv University demonstrated the amazing correlation between an individual's level of religiosity and that individual's right wing political leanings. In their study, a 100% of those who identified themselves as *charedi* (ultra-Orthodox, or more politically correct, fervently religious) identified themselves as right wing politically. 81.3% of those that identified themselves as religious (for the most part, Modern Zionist Orthodox) identified themselves as right wing politically, whereas only 22% of those that identified themselves as secular identified themselves as rightists. More recently, for instance, the peace index conducted by the Steinmentz Institute in May 2000 indicates that only 28% of the *charedi* and 46% of the non-*charedi* religious respondents supported the unilateral withdrawal from Lebanon, as compared with 73% of the secular. In July of 2000, 72% of those that voted for the *charedi* United Torah Judaism party, and 62% of those that voted for Shas, held the view that Barak was excessively conciliatory in the Camp David Summit, compared to a majority among the secular who held the view that the positions held were appropriate. As to the future of Jewish settlements as part of a final agreement with the Palestinians, 72% of the *charedi* opposed any uprooting of settlements, compared to 25.2% who hold this view among secular Israeli Jews.

Ehud Barak's election was not based on his peace policy, but rather, his perceived commitment to shifting priorities and addressing domestic ailments, particularly in the areas of religion and state. It was Barak's popular campaign for equal military draft of yeshiva students, and his campaign slogans "Money for education and not for fictitious (religious) organizations," referring to the wide corruption uncovered with regard to state allocations to yeshivas and other Orthodox organizations, that insured his victory. Fed up with a government that bends over backwards for the religious parties, it was only natural to see the thousands of Barak's supporters streaming to Rabin Square in Tel Aviv on the night the elections results were announced, shouting and waving banners pleading "Just not Shas, Just not Shas." They expressed the yearnings of the majority in Israel for a government free of these coercive pressures, one that would pursue a civic agenda, strengthen democracy, and step up policies for greater economic justice. Alas, Barak's true agenda soon became evident to the Israeli public. In his total commitment to the peace process he turned his back on his supporters, choosing to focus instead on forming an impossible coalition that would include both Mafdal, (the National Religious Party) and Shas (the ultra-Orthodox Sephardi party). The fact that United Torah Judaism (Agudah and Degel Hatorah) did not join his coalition did not prevent him from reaching tacit understandings with them and making concessions in order to secure their neutrality, if not support.

It seemed to many, including myself, an impossible mission. After undermining the public's hope for a government that is free of corruption, he then found that he could not count on the support of the religious parties for his peace initiatives when the successful resolution of the peace process rested on their votes. He and his senior staff operated under the illusion that their votes could be bought by turning a blind eye to the abuse of authority and funds as was demonstrated in the controversy over Shas' educational network, "*maayan hachinuch hatorani*," which led to Minister of Education Yossi Sarid's resignation.

Realizing that doing his best may not have been enough, Barak began recently to reassess the public sentiments that have won him the election, and concluded that his chances lie in spinning public discourse and highlighting once again the issues of religion and state. A surprise initiative for a "Civil Revolution" that some described as a "Secular Revolution," was the result of this reassessment. Cynics have suggested that this was a ploy to win back the support of some of the religious parties who would be willing to give him further slack in order to get rid of this imminent threat. If so, then Barak may have misread their motivation as well as the endurance of his supporters.

Barak failed to acknowledge that the majority of Shas' constituency identifies with the right wing. Shas' dramatic growth and its ability to benefit from the new system that separated the vote for prime minister and the vote for the Knesset lists was based on their ability to draw supporters from the Likkud, primarily manipulating ethnic Sephardic frustrations, and inducing them to vote for Shas. This transfer of votes, however, did not change their core political identity, and in heart and mind, they remain Likkudniks. Ovadia Yosef is well aware that even had he wanted to sanction a generous peace policy, he could stretch the line only so much. At this point, the extent of Yosef's commitment to peace is ambiguous, as is the extent to which he is willing to go back to his past statements about giving up territory as religiously and halachically justified for the sake of Pikuah Nefesh (saving of lives). In more recent statements, Yosef seems to have altered his position, apparently having arrived at the conclusion that giving up territory will further endanger Jewish lives and thereby reversing his seemingly peace driven ruling of the past.

In the Ashkenazi ultra-Orthodox camp, similar sentiments about territorial concessions and the absolute sanctity of Jerusalem were also voiced by the political and rabbinical authorities. While in the past there was a mistaken perception that these groups support peace with neighboring nations, it is now evident that the intrinsic right wing nationalistic tendencies and the distrust, if not hatred of Arabs, is the decisive factor in their political maneuvering.

Barak's overestimation of the support that he could muster for his peace initiatives held equally true in regards to the Modern Zionist Orthodox position, despite the fact that their position on the process was made explicit from the outset. Their message that they would stay in until the moment any territorial compromise and uprooting of settlements is further contemplated was unequivocal. We must remember that for this camp, the religious authority still emanates from the former Chief Rabbis of Israel Rabbi Avraham Shapira, and Rabbi Mordechai Eliahu. Both of them have for years been know for their uncompromising views on territorial questions and the settlements. They have joined together only recently for a widely publicized call to men, women, and children to gather together for a public worship and outcry for the "sanctity and wholeness of Jerusalem and the land of Israel and the security of its inhabitants" at the Western Wall. The prayer and outcry, according to the ad, are intended to void and interfere with the attempt of those who are trying to "rob and hand over our inheritance of the holy land to murderers." It was Rabbi Avraham Shapira who joined together in the past with other notable Modern Zionist rabbis in a rabbinic edict addressed at army soldiers to disobey their officers when ordered to vacate Hebron. What is not always understood is that this position does not only reflect Rabbi Shapira's and like-minded rabbinic authorities' view on the territories and peace, but also their attitude towards democracy and the character of Israel as a Jewish and democratic state. In a widely distributed response to a Knesset Member query on the relationship between halacha and democracy, rabbi Shapira responded that " there is no conflict between democracy and halacha" but then qualified his statement, adding that "the only limit, in terms of the Jewish law, to the authority of the elected members of the Knesset, is that they may not make any decisions in contravention to the halacha." Let there be no misunderstanding that when it comes to questions such as the territories, Shapira and his colleagues are determined to de-legitimize any conflicting view even when it is offered by other rabbinic authorities such as Rabbi Amital of the Meimad Orthodox Peace Movement.

The conclusion must be fully understood. The political religious force in Israel has been an anti peace force and it is in the interest of those who wish to promote peace to recognize the need to find ways of abating that force. On the other hand, joining in the struggle for religious freedom and pluralism in Israel and strengthening the hand of the non-Orthodox is a move that will strengthen the prospects of peace. Peace and ultimately Israel's democratic character depend on our ability to overcome past complaisance over the unholy alliance of religion and state in Israel.

As this article is written, the weekly torah portion is, appropriately, "the Life of Sarah." The week's parsha fills us with hope as we see that while the relationship of Isaac and Ishmael, and the mothers, Sarah and Hagar were plagued by crises and at times violence, with the death of Abraham the brothers find a way to unite, as sons of the same father, just as the Jews and the Arabs will ultimately unite. After all, in our tradition "the deeds of the father are symbols to his sons."

Uri Regev was ordained by HUC-JIR in Jerusalem in 1986. He is also an attorney. As the Director of the Israel Religious Action Center of the Israel Movement for Progressive Judaism, Rabbi Regev is the leading spokesperson for religious pluralism and individual rights in Israel.

CAUSING REASONED REACTIONS

Judith S. Lewis

One of the goals that has emerged as part of the mission of Temple Israel is to bridge the gap – or what appears to be more of an abyss these days – between what is going on in the academic world and the synagogue. Pulpit rabbis generally don't have the kind of time required to devote to the thorough research required to answer certain questions definitively, or reason through new ideas. Academics often do not participate fully in the life of Reform synagogues out of a sense of intellectual dissatisfaction or frustration. At Temple Israel, through the Adler Seminar on Modern Judaism, and other ongoing programs, we have attempted to integrate cutting-edge scholarly insights with our practices and rituals.

If, however, you were to ask the average, Jewishly connected, New Yorker where the most exciting action was taking place in the modern, progressive Jewish world, they might point to B'nai Jeshurun, or perhaps make reference to Synagogue 2000. An issue of *Reform Judaism*, the publication of the Union of American Hebrew Congregations, that same publication that featured Rabbi Richard Levy kissing his *tzitzit* on the cover of the issue that first introduced the Statement of Principles, was devoted to Synagogue 2000 efforts to transform the market oriented synagogue into a vibrant community of spiritually active participants.

Their goals are certainly worthwhile and important. A congregation full of involved, connected, knowledgeable, practicing Jews is a good thing. Especially if we want to raise children who identify positively with the Jewish community, we have to provide that kind of atmosphere. It is the only way to condition them to feel at home within Judaism, to make Jewishness an essential part of their self-perception. When it comes to children, I suspect that may be the only way to get anywhere near guaranteeing them a healthy Jewish identity as adults. We definitely must proceed, as a movement, on that front. Nevertheless, what is missing from these spirited, warm, vibrant Jewish communities is the philosophical foundation – the "why." What does modern Judaism offer that makes a synagogue a better place to find connection, comfort, inspiration, than, say, a country club. Why is it preferable to join a Torah study minyan and spend Saturday morning deeply engaged in a heated discussion of the weekly portion, than, say, to play tennis, or golf, or better yet relax together with one's whole family discussing the events of the past week over a sumptuous brunch? It comes down to the old push-pin versus poetry debate and not only do the majority of my congregants opt for push-pin, but given the kinds of activities some of them engage in all week long, including philanthropic and political *"tikkun olam"* – world repairing – I can't come up with a reasonable motive to persuade them otherwise. Other than b'nai mitzvah, baby-naming, and other life-cycle celebrations, I can't seem to come up with a sufficiently compelling reason for those with attractive leisure alternatives to attend Sabbath morning services.

The greatest contributing historical factor to the lack of Jewish commitment today was not the reason and science part of the Enlightenment. It was the resulting emancipation, the loss of legal self-governance and political isolation. Until relatively recently in America, anti-Semitism and the effects of psychological conditioning seemed to keep even classical reform synagogues full on Sabbath mornings (even where the Sabbath was celebrated on Sunday.) The last few generations of unbridled American assimilation opportunities have destroyed even those internal psychological commitments. The statistic that concerns me more than any number about intermarriage is that 58% of the Jewish population has no affiliation with any Jewish institution or community. What concerns me most about that statistic is that many of those unaffiliated are among the brightest, most successful, most committed to values I would consider Jewishly desirable. Many of them have precisely the attributes that would most contribute to a productive Jewish future.

So, while transforming synagogue participation *ala* Synagogue 2000 creates vital, vibrant "spiritual" communities, many congregants and potential congregants first need to understand why they should be part of a synagogue community. Before we work on preserving Jewish identity, we need to be able to articulate what Jewish identity is, and why it is worth preserving.

Let me share an ordinary weekend in the life of a pulpit rabbi. I officiated at three weddings, and we only officiate at weddings of members and their families! One was between two individuals born as Jews; one in our own congregation, the other raised in conservative and orthodox synagogues. The second wedding was between a woman raised in a liberal Protestant home, who converted to Judaism and married a man raised in a traditional Jewish home, but for the past several years an active member of this congregation. The groom in the last wedding was the grandson of a Yitshak Elhanan Seminary graduate who left to become a socialist, and an ardent liberal Zionist father with all sorts of American civil rights movement credentials and lots of Yiddishists in his background. The bride was a non-practicing Muslim woman from Turkey who had undertaken serious study of Judaism (with a conservative rabbi) but has not yet had time to go through a formal conversion process.

There is no question that all three couples will raise Jewish children and create Jewish homes, but if I had to place bets, the couple who will have the most difficulty navigating that endeavor is the one where both partners were born Jewish. Only their families expressed any sense of religious incompatibility.

Obviously, this is only anecdotal evidence, but it is consistent enough with my experience over the past twenty years to identify various trends. Jews in America are not a distinct, homogeneous ethnic group and of course never have been. The diversity within the liberal Jewish community, however, has become much more profound in the past generation, through intermarriage and conversion. The antagonisms and distrust between various factions within the overall Jewish community are far more intense than any tension between liberal Jews and liberal non-Jews. People who convert to Reform Judaism do not expect to become part of an ethnic group. They enter the Jewish group to share its values, its theology, its customs and rituals, its past and its future. Those whose Jewishness is largely an ethnic identity even find themselves becoming more religious – in the sense of sharing a commitment to a set of values, a theology, and a religious calendar – in order to build a home with a spouse not born into Judaism.

So what is the content of that modern Jewish religious identity?

It is not, at least at the outset, the Statement of Principles image of standing together at Sinai. That may emerge as a sentimentally effective metaphor when a convert stands before the open ark, with the Torah in his or her arms, to recite the Sh'ma and receive a Hebrew name of ben or bat Avraham v'Sarah. But it is not the practical, motivating content of the average, educated adult who leads an observant Reform Jewish life, whether from birth or by choice.

I would argue that the identity of the well-educated, successful, emotionally healthy, observant Reform Jew consists of a belief, even a leap of faith, if you will, that the content of Judaism is consistent with the content of scientific truth and the structure of reality. Further, that individual sees a Jewish religious life as a way to appreciate and promote those values within his or her family, to give human life meaning consistent with scientific truth and the reality of experience. It is not the origin – whether truth revealed at Sinai or conclusion drawn from evidence, but the objective – a life of value and meaning, that keeps practicing Reform Jews Jewish. The problem is, fewer and fewer people are receiving that faith because Reform leadership has failed to keep up with scientific truth and the reality of human experience. Let me confess, here, that I am an elitist. I am fully aware that approximately 90% of any congregation cares very little about the why, the philosophical foundation of their religious community. They want a bar mitzvah. They want Joey to be raised Jewish, and they respond to the Synagogue 2000 spirituality because it feeds the real emotional needs of most of today's families. My remarks are intended for those who hope change the future, to steer a course for Judaism that will be creative, living, and productive for future generations.

As Robert Seltzer stated in *Jewish People, Jewish Thought* (p.757), "like every living religion, Judaism is a frame of reference for apprehending the ultimate and for participating in a community formed by and constantly re-forming a sacred tradition. Jewish thought is an effort to present Jewish teaching in a theoretically consistent manner. Each such effort eventually passes into history where is awaits the historian, but the articulation remains a perpetual task if Judaism is still to be a viable spiritual form." I would add that Judaism has always depended on diversity of opinions, radical diversity, and Reform Judaism experimented with radical responses to the new experience of modernity. Some of them were mistakes; others managed to keep Judaism alive. But it seems we have dropped the task of experimenting, of creating in the present generations. My hope is that some small group will take up this task again. It will not necessarily be felt by our children, or even our grandchildren, but it will provide a new outer limit against which they can react to find an appropriate middle ground, a modern, viable, living Judaism.

In 1995, Ismar Schorsch, chancellor of the Jewish Theological Seminary published a monograph entitled *Sacred Cluster: The Core Values of Conservative Judaism*, (www.JTSA.edu) outlining seven fundamental tenets of Conservative Judaism. Interestingly, each one of those core values was a direct and conscious response or reaction to founding principles of Reform Judaism, as well as a reasoned rejection of orthodox doctrine. I would like to go through the seven core values for those of you who are not familiar with the text, to demonstrate what, in 1995, Schorsch perceived as normative Reform Judaism.

He begins by explaining that he has identified three national core values and three religious core values, with one overarching theological core value – arriving conveniently at the sacred number of seven. These are:
1. The Centrality of Modern Israel
2. Hebrew: The Irreplaceable Language of Jewish Expression
3. Devotion to the Ideal of *Klal Yisrael*
4. The Defining Role of Torah in the Reshaping of Judaism
5. The Study of Torah
6. The Governance of Jewish Life by *Halakha*
7. Belief in God

In his discussion of The Centrality of Modern Israel, Schorsch explains that "the thrust of Conservative Judaism was not to denationalize Judaism" – clearly a response to the early Reform definition of Judaism as exclusively a faith or religion. Then he refers to Zacharias Frankel's break with Reform over the issue of Hebrew at the Frankfurt Rabbinical Conference in 1845 in his discussion of Hebrew: The Irreplaceable Language of Jewish Expression. He records that "despite the leniency of Jewish law, [Frankel] was not prepared to endorse a resolution which would acknowledge that synagogue services could theoretically dispense with Hebrew. Given the rapid shrinkage of Judaism with the advent of emancipation, the fostering of Hebrew for Frankel became a symbol of historical continuity and national unity" (in direct contrast, of course, to Reform's rejection of Judaism as a nationality and its embrace of the Diaspora and its vernacular).

In Schorsch's section on Devotion to the Ideal of *Klal Yisrael,* he contends that Conservative Jews give more generally and more exclusively to Jewish causes than Reform Jews who dilute their philanthropy with secular causes. "Such admirable commitment to the welfare of the whole does not spring from any special measure of ethnicity, as is so often ascribed to Conservative Jews" he states. "Rather, I would argue that it is nurtured by the acute historical sense cultivated by their leadership. In opposition to exclusively rational, moral or halahkic criteria for change, Conservative Judaism embraced a historical romanticism that rooted tradition in the normative power of a heroic past."

In his fourth value, The Defining Role of Torah in the Reshaping of Judaism, Schorsch distinguishes between the divinity of the Torah, and its sanctity, calling it "the foundation text of Judaism, the apex of an inverted pyramid of infinite commentary, not because it is divine, but because it is sacred, that is, adopted by the Jewish people as its spiritual font. The term skirts the divisive and futile question of origins, the fetid swamp of heresy. The sense of individual obligation, of being commanded, does not derive from divine authorship, but communal consent. The Written Torah, no less than the Oral Torah, reverberates with the divine-human encounter, with a minimum of revelation and a maximum of interpretation." In contrast to Reform's traditional elevation of the Torah as the only divinely inspired text of Jewish tradition, and rabbinic commentary strictly a record of Judaism's evolution in response to changing historical circumstance, Schorsch makes the entire body of Jewish literature an encounter with the divine.

Similarly, when he discusses The Study of Torah he states that "the full meaning of sacred texts will always elude those who restrict the range of acceptable questions, fear to read contextually and who engage in willful ignorance" – that is, neither Reform, nor orthodox readings. He continues, "what Conservative Judaism brings to this ancient and unfinished dialectic are the tools and perspectives of modern scholarship blended with traditional learning and empathy. It is precisely the sacredness of these texts that requires of serious students to employ every piece of scholarly equipment to unpack their contents. Their power is crippled by inflicting upon them readings that no longer carry any intellectual cogency. Modern Jews deserve the right to study Torah in consonance with their mental world and not solely through the eyes of their ancestors. Judaism does not seek to limit our thinking, only our actions…. It is not the tools of the trade that make philology or history or anthropology or feminist studies threatening, but the spirit in which they are applied."

The sixth core value is the governance of Jewish life by *halakha*. Schorsch observes that Conservative Jews are rabbinic and not biblical Jews – in contrast to early Reform, which turned to the Torah and Prophets as our primary inspiration. Conservative Jews avow the sanctity of the Oral Torah erected by Rabbinic Judaism alongside the Written Torah as complementary and vital to deepen, enrich and transform it.

> "Even if in their individual lives they may often fall short on observance, they generally do not ask of their rabbinic leadership to dismantle wholesale the entire halakhic system in order to translate personal behavior into public policy [like same-sex marriages or patrilineal descent]. Imbued with devotion to *klal yisrael* and a pervasive respect for tradition, they are more inclined to sacrifice personal autonomy for a reasonable degree of consensus and uniformity in communal life.

> The *halakhic* system, historically considered, evinces a constant pattern of responsiveness, change and variety. Conservative Judaism did not read that record as carte blanche for a radical revision or even rejection of the system, but rather as warrant for valid adjustment where absolutely necessary. The result is a body of Conservative law sensitive to human need, halakhic integrity and the worldwide character of the Jewish community. Due deliberation generally avoided the adoption of positions which turned out to be ill-advised and unacceptable.

Interestingly, here Reform has actually served its intended purpose, pushing Conservative to follow on certain major issues such as the ordination of women, and this paragraph, of the entire monograph, captures the polemic of conservative versus reform: "what is critical for the present crisis is the reaffirmation of *halakha* as a bulwark against syncretism, the overwhelming of Judaism by American society, not by coercion but seduction. Judaism is not a quilt of random patches onto which anything might be sewn. Its extraordinary individuality is marked by integrity and coherence. The supreme function of *halakha* (and Hebrew, for that matter) is to replace external barriers with internal ones, to create the private space in which Jews can cultivate their separate identities while participating in the open society that engulfs them."

Aside from the mildly pejorative reference to a patchwork Judaism, in other words, Reform Judaism -- also referred to twenty years ago by Gene Borowitz as "Jewish Catalogue" Judaism, this is, indeed, a cogent and legitimate definition for a modern, liberal Judaism.

Theoretically, the Reform position might have been that Jewish practice should enable Jews to cultivate their distinct identity in ways that are consistent with, and viable within the society in which we live.

And finally...in regard to the insufficiency of the Reform view of God, Schorsch says of his overarching core value, Belief in God that, "Jewish tradition continues unbroken in Conservative Judaism, where yearning for God wells up primarily not from reason or revelation but from the blood-soaked, value-laden and textually rooted historical experience of the Jewish people." I don't know where Schorsch puts Maimonides, within Jewish tradition, but I don't think of his God as particularly blood-soaked.

I might feel defensive about Professor Schorsch's reactions to classical Reform positions, if Reform Judaism still embraced any one of those positions. But Reform has backed away from almost every one of those principles and values to which Schorsch felt it necessary to react. What troubles me today is that we offer no coherent philosophical positions against which Conservative Judaism can react – which is, by definition, what conservatives are supposed to do. Reformers should be breaking new ground, offering risky new concepts that challenge traditionalists. We should be plunging into secular culture to look for ideas that we can borrow, try on, and dress up in Jewish garb. We should be making mistakes and taking chances, but instead we have folded, regressed, and surrendered to the majority. Conservative Jews have infiltrated Reform congregations where they may "in their individual lives ...fall short on observance" as Schorsch put it, without the guilt. Philosophically Reform Jews feel abandoned and disappointed. True, reason and rationality may have lost their power in the postmodern world, but empirical scientific research has not. Modern brain science may have dissected Hermann Cohen's fellow feeling and explained it as evolutionary survival wiring, but if Jewish literature is an accurate record of a particular human group's experience and collective wisdom, then surely there is room here to create a new context for interpreting traditional texts. But where is the leadership of our movement trying to incorporate new knowledge and insights into our heritage?

CAUSING REASONED REACTION

There is a great deal of work going on in the world of science and religion. There are two major styles of science and religion dialogue – one that asks, "what does science tell us about the structure of the universe, and how does this relate to what our ancestors once called God?" The other uses scientific discoveries to "prove" the accuracy of a dogma or text. You are probably familiar with the Templeton Foundation, and perhaps with the work of the Center for Theology and the Natural Sciences. I have tried to find similar efforts in the Jewish world. Stephen Jay Gould has touched on the subject, and I believe decided that the two should remain separate spheres. Many Jewish authorities are struggling with the ethical issues presented by new developments in medicine and health care, with ecological crises, privacy issues raised by technology, and so forth, trying to apply traditional texts and values to radically new circumstances. And then there are those in the orthodox world who try to demonstrate the truth of Torah by proving that modern scientific discoveries verify traditional texts. The book *Old Wine New Flasks, Reflections on Science and Jewish Tradition*, a record of correspondence between Roald Hoffman, a professor of Chemistry at Cornell, and Shira Leibowitz Schmidt, a former engineer and now orthodox mother of six, living in Israel, is an excellent example of the genre.

What I have been unable to locate is the first kind of theology happening in the Jewish world, the kind the founders of Reform Judaism were doing when they applied Wissenschaft to Judaism. Where are the secular scholars, physicists, economists, biologists, psychologists, who have an equivalent command of modern Jewish knowledge?

One of the problems seems to be that some of the leading experts doing the most groundbreaking original scientific research are the very kind of Jews we would rely upon to place their discoveries in a Jewish context. Yet because they are of the generation that was so thoroughly assimilated, they have no familiarity with any modern Jewish context, no religious vocabulary. Freud was, perhaps, an early example of this problem, from a previous generation. And Einstein too, though he seemed much more articulate about the theological implications of his work. Religious practice had been devalued in their lives by the rationality and scientific passion of their day. Because Jewishness, while an ethnic attribute of some ambivalence, was thoroughly and securely a part of who they were, they felt little need to articulate a connection between the faith of their ancestors and the discoveries of their own labors. Science was their religion. Jewish was their personal identity.

    I do believe that there is a connection between the nature of certain scientific theory and what I would consider core Jewish concepts – the unity of the creator, the emphasis on the perceived world, the recognition that tension exists within every living system. I am suggesting that it is time for Jewish religious leadership to start reinterpreting traditional texts in the light of modern knowledge. We don't need to prove the truth of those texts, but to give our children connections from their heritage that make sense in the context of their intellectual reality.

    In the early days of Reform, leading rabbis were valued at least as much for their secular scholarship as for their Jewish learning. The great Reform rabbis of the first half of the last century couldn't always make it through a page of Talmud, but they were widely respected as serious secular thinkers, philosophers, members of the intelligentsia. They were supported and trusted by their lay people, especially the merchants and businessmen, to represent them in the gentile, upper middle class, educated world – to give upwardly mobile Jews the respectability and acceptability they were insecure about obtaining on their own. Reform rabbis were expected to interpret Judaism to the gentiles as consistent with the noblest values and commitments of American society. That was the Reform Judaism that gave birth to Conservative Judaism, and the Reform Judaism to which Schorsch's Core Values react.

Too many congregants – or potential congregants – today have more sophisticated knowledge of their particular field of expertise or profession than the average Reform rabbi even has about Judaism. Some congregants know more about Judaism as well. Not every Reform Temple is blessed as we are with a president who can quote Pirke Avot or who reads Josephus for fun, but there are thousands of yeshiva-schooled individuals out there who might find, in a renewed Reform Judaism, a reasonable substitute for radical apikorsus or complete rejection of Judaism altogether.

But modern secular scholars who happen to be Jewish, by in large, do not have access to, or interest in serious, scientific Jewish study, while there are plenty of Orthodox scientists who have found creative ways of living in both worlds at once

Modern, professional, well-educated, non-orthodox American Jews should not have to be satisfied with a pre-enlightenment reading of traditional texts. The challenge is to transmit the serious study of texts that is happening in the universities into the Reform synagogue so that the people who could be creating new, challenging, provocative, experimental paths for the future have reasonable access to the past.

We should be reading texts in historical context to understand how our ancestors adapted to their diverse circumstances. We should also be asking our congregants to share the knowledge of their disciplines to apply to our knowledge of Jewish history. And we need to make our synagogues and our religion more credible to people who are experts in their fields, who are the brightest and the best of society.

In this country, I do not think *halacha*, as a separate body of religious law, will ever be compelling to the majority of modern American Jews. It is an American ideal not to live under religious authority. From a historical perspective, though, Judaism is also a collection of texts. Each text became normative only in the generations after it was written. Various texts compete for authority during the lifetime of their authors, and enjoy varying levels of influence, but a text only becomes part of our religious canon when the period of its creation has come to a radical end.

I do not know whether the modern period has come to a radical end or not, or if the end is near or far. I do know that the computer revolution has to have as profound an impact on our history as the moveable type printing press did. We might search for some clue to the future Jewish canon in the internet – the metaphor of a web with various interconnected sites linked by some common element. But the development of the computer itself is a sufficiently radical change in our text technology to mark a radical transition in the modern period. There is, for example, a new handheld medical database device into which physicians can enter a set of symptoms and receive suggested diagnoses, recommended treatments, and predicted outcomes. For years, lucky patients relied on the art of brilliant diagnosis. More recently, the health insurance crisis has made it virtually impossible for the great diagnosticians to prosper. Now technology has produced a device that may make it possible for even a poorly trained, unskilled physician to treat challenging cases more successfully. Robotic and computer controlled surgery are similarly changing the face of modern medicine, not to mention the economic pressures that have developed in a generation.

The computer has enabled humans to capture an increasingly complex body of information. E. O. Wilson's *Consilience* examines some of the implications of our revolutionary ability to track complexity. He has also written: "we have come to the crucial stage in the history of biology when religion itself is subject to the explanations of the natural sciences... sociobiology can account for the very origin of mythology by the principle of natural selection acting on the genetically evolving material structure of the human brain. If this interpretation is correct, the final decisive edge enjoyed by scientific naturalism will come from its capacity to explain traditional religion, its chief competitor, as a wholly material phenomenon. Theology is not likely to survive as an independent intellectual discipline. But religion itself will endure for a long time as a vital force in society." (CTNS Newsletter)

In other words, our ability to capture and record the subtle data of minds, of society, of evolution demonstrates the biological origins of that which we call religion. I think it has always been Judaism's genius to transform itself into something else as soon as its previous function has been usurped by something else – whether it was Roman rule, Emancipation, or perhaps now science. Wilson sees religion's utility, although he regards it as nothing more than a survival-strategy, which has become embedded in our genes. And Judaism is uniquely poised to survive because it is not a religion exclusively or even primarily. It is and always has been a response to human need. As such, it contains elements of faith and belief, because humans are biologically programmed to need faith and belief.

I see at least two possible scenarios for where progressive, modern, post-enlightenment Judaism should be headed. One is that we remain on a continuum; that Reform, or whatever we call the successor to what provoked the Conservative movement into existence, continues pushing the envelope, pulling outward toward our host culture, for conservative forces to react to. Or, in the eventuality of some major crisis or end to this particular golden age, a new structure of Judaism will emerge that can sustain a national identity.

What we have stopped doing is synthesizing the discoveries of modern culture with the insights of our tradition. We have stopped taking chances. Let me mention, just for a moment, the recent resolution of the CCAR to support a rabbi's right to perform same-sex marriages. A great deal of ink – or more accurately pixels – were spilled debating the *kedusha* of same sex marriages. To my knowledge, no one stopped to ask what this *kedusha* concept is really all about. Are we still in the business of acquiring exclusive use of another human being? Why do we even still use that term for heterosexual marriages? The current monogamous nuclear family structure seems, from statistical evidence, to be going through some major upheaval. Maybe the whole institution needs to be radically re-evaluated. Where is the leadership coming to help us form new family structures that respond more effectively to the new circumstances of modern society? The reactionary call for family values is a response to a disintegration of traditional roles, not to a conscious effort to redefine family values that actually work effectively given the realities of society. Instead, it should be a response to thoughtful, experimental, conscious attempts to create new forms of family life. And the raw material – the psychology, and brain science, the economic theory and urban planning – is all out there. But we have sealed ourselves off from it, and look only to the past, trying to apply old solutions to new problems.

The availability of information, and the speed of acquiring it has increased dramatically – but human brain capacity and function evolves at a much slower pace. We are no more able to grasp complexity and understand the magnitude of that complexity. The human mind will probably never to be able to command any significant segment of that complexity, but the computer can, which means that computers may someday occupy the role of priests, professionals, of the canon – they give us power that no human mind can reproduce, and yet they can never actually reproduce the complexity of a human – without becoming human, which is too scary a thought to contemplate. At the same time, the more we know about the world, the more we realize how insignificant we are in it.

Reform or progressive Judaism should be seeking the

CAUSING REASONED REACTION

latest scientific insights outside of Judaism and applying them to guidance about proper human conduct. We have to go back to the basic questions: what is the nature of the human being, what is the purpose of life, how do we distinguish good and evil, what is justice and what is the source of human cruelty, destruction, and devastation? We have to look at brain science, chaos theory, cosmology. We have to embrace the products of scientific research with courage, even when they tell us that we are cosmically insignificant accidents of energy. And then we have to create a Jewish form, because Judaism allows us to act as if human life matters by positing the Oneness of the Creator – as a statement of faith – always a step beyond the grasp of scientific knowledge.

You are probably familiar with the little Chasidic adage that says, keep two truths in your pocket, and take them out according to the need of the moment. Let one be: "for my sake was the world created" and the other "I am dust and ashes."

That is the essence of Judaism – the tension between realities. Two opposites can be true at the same time, and Jews have been conditioned by Jewish history to tolerate that paradox, without having to posit a theology that defies scientific evidence. Even scientific theory seems to support and confirm the wisdom of our ancestors. Let me suggest a sort of quantum mechanics interpretation of the well-known passage attributed to Rabbi Tarfon in Pirke Avot:

lo aleycha ham'lacha l'gmor, v'lo atah ben chorin l'hibatel mimena

One can never actually complete any discrete task, because the system is infinite and in constant flux, yet no matter what we choose to do, or not to do, it is impossible to avoid having an impact on that system.

Reform Judaism, historically, was a force for change and adaptation. It was a powerful enough force to provoke the development of both Orthodox Judaism in Germany in the 19th Century, and Conservative Judaism as in this country at the turn of the 20th Century as reactions to its innovations. If Reform Judaism ceases to exert that kind of force on contemporary Jewish thought, it ceases to perform its function as a creative, vibrant interpretation of living Judaism. It will still influence the course of Jewish history, by its sheer numbers and success in this country. Reform Judaism, however, may lose its relevance to the very Jews who have the most to offer to future generations.

It is no joke that for every two Jews there are three opinions. Rather, it is the secret of our survival. We are facing a true crisis when the most liberal of the Jewish movements lacks the intellectual vision to arouse controversy and debate with our more conservative branches. By continuing the dialogue between scholars and rabbis, the academy and the synagogue, the scientist and the philosopher, we may regain the courage to experiment, to make mistakes, and to prepare the next generation to embrace its history.

Judith S. Lewis was ordained by HUC-JIR in 1980. She is the rabbi of Temple Israel of the City of New York.